Mother's Seventh Daughter

Violet Carol Foot

ARTHUR H. STOCKWELL LTD
Torrs Park, Ilfracombe, Devon, EX34 8BA
Established 1898
www.ahstockwell.co.uk

By the same author:

Sixteen Shillings and Tuppence Ha'penny (paperback), Minerva Press, 2001; (large print, hardback), Magna Large Print, 2003

Emily's Seventh Daughter (private limited edition), Arthur H. Stockwell Ltd, 2003

Both written under the name of Violet Frederick Foot.

ISBN 978-0-7223-4912-0
Printed in Great Britain by
Arthur H. Stockwell Ltd
Torrs Park   Ilfracombe
Devon EX34 8BA

In loving memory of our mother and respect for all she endured in giving birth to her ten singly born daughters and in raising them to be good, clean, respectable loving wives and mothers themselves.

"... Come my friends,
'Tis not too late
to seek a newer world..."

ULYSSES

ACKNOWLEDGEMENTS

Firstly, I would like to thank my publisher and his staff for their excellent communication with me, which makes me very happy.

My sisters, Emmie, Matilda, Eileen and Doreen for their contributions, photos and interest in my book.

The heads and teachers of both of my schools for the good grounding and teachings turning me into a well-rounded adult and helping to make my life happy and fulfilled.

All the Old Hares of our yesteryears for the loan or contribution of school photos.

All who have allowed me to add them to my roll of honour on the addendum pages.

There was no room for any more, my sincere apologies.

Mr Michael Coggins for info on my family tree.

The RNID Library for the Medresco pictures.

Special mention to Elaine, Rosa, Jenny, Ian, Ronald, Donald, Barry and Valerie (W.) who keep in touch with me by emails. I love communicating with everyone, especially as we are mostly in our eighties.

Thank you also to Mr Bees Fotostop, Downham Market, Norfolk, for good communication and copies of family photos. I have no idea who took many of them and I regret I am unable to show acknowledgements. They were taken a very long time ago – the coloured group photo of sisters was taken in 1973 (see page 87) and the black-and-white group photo was taken in March 1947 (see page 71).

CHAPTER ONE

In Mother's later years I once asked her jokingly, "Would you have married Father if it hadn't been a shotgun wedding, Mum?"

Mother laughed till tears ran down her face. "You must be joking, Vie."

Our mother, Emily, married our father, Albert, at St Dunstan's Church in Limehouse, London. They were sixteen and nineteen years of age respectively. A copy of the marriage certificate showed they both raised their ages to twenty-one years.

The first seven of their ten singly born daughters were born in London, the first, Emmie, on Mother's seventeenth birthday.

Father died senile in 1991 and Mother died of thrombosis and possibly a heart attack in 1994. We have a copy of Mother's post-mortem and a copy of Father's death certificate. There was no post-mortem; he was in a nursing home.

Mother's parents were long-lived. Granny was eighty-seven, Grandad well into his nineties and he chewed tobacco all his life.

I have no recollection of our paternal grandparents. Our three eldest sisters did and they did not like them.

At fifteen years of age Mother helped teach Sunday school at the Mission in Limehouse to the ragamuffin shoeless (in many instances) children of the poverty-stricken hopelessly poor parents who abounded. Such poor souls were caught up in the depression years of the 1920s, when men returned who had briefly and valiantly fought for our glorious country in the First World War – the Great War to end all wars, the terrible Somme, Dardanelles, Ypres et al. Now there was no work for these proud men. There were no generous social-security benefits as in modern times. Do not misunderstand – I meant generous compared to nowadays. There was no National Health Service; you had to pay for a doctor or go to a charity.

It was now the time of the monstrously long dole queues, where men had to queue outside the labour exchange to their shame. It was not really shameful, but as previously valued members of His Majesty King George's military they felt so wretched it is hard to imagine what was going through their minds. The war to end all wars! They gave up their youth and, like the older men who followed, they laid down their lives for king and country only to end up all but starving had it not been for charity.

The East End of London was well known for its pearly kings and queens with their clothes stitched all over with 'pearl' buttons in wonderful patterns of great ingenuity.

Extended families of brothers, sisters and cousins lived cheek by jowl in the same areas all in the same boat. Poverty with a capital P.

It was the years of the Great Depression when Mother gave birth to eight of her ten daughters, from 1924 to 1937, all singly born.

My other parents, my wartime foster-parents, Alice and Bill, nurtured me from age four to nine and a half years of age. I loved them dearly all my life and their way of life was as different from the Cockneys of London as the proverbial chalk and cheese. Bill was a coal miner and so were most of the males of that generation. They had not long been married and I was their pride and joy, Alice's living doll.

Our mother was born in Bethnal Green; Father was born in Limehouse.

Our maternal grandparents, Granny and Grandad, also had a large brood of their own. Grandad drove a horse and cart and was known as a carman. They were a very lovely, friendly little couple and had very long lives. Like most people they loved eating brains, lights, pigs' trotters, tripe (known as plain and purl), pig's head, liver, and soups made from bones and vegetables – all the cheapest food which they could aspire to find the means to purchase.

Granny died of malnutrition aged eighty-seven; nobody knew why – she just suddenly stopped eating.

Father's parents wed at St Simon Zelotes Church, Bethnal Green, London. Father's mother already had a son when she married his father. She then gave birth six more times. The much loved brother of Father, Tom, whose photo he carried in his wallet all his adult life, was Private 421465, 'D' Coy, 2nd/10th Battalion, London Regiment. He died on 17 July 1918. Tom is buried at Pernois British Cemetery, Halloy-les-Pernois, Somme, France, 11 E 19. He was only twenty-one years old.

George, another brother, Able Seaman C/JX160440, HMS *Waverley*, Royal Navy, died on 30 May in the Second World War. He was thirty-eight years old. The memorial for the *Waverley* sailors is at the Chatham Naval Memorial, Kent, grave 35.3. The memorial overlooks the town of Chatham. It is approached by a steep path from the Town Hall Gardens.

To escape from his overly strict mother, Father often took to sleeping rough in the fields. Mr Edwards, a lifelong friend of our family, told me that in 1976. Consequently Father suffered from chest pains all his life until his death. He was in and out of Oldchurch Hospital for bronchitis and pleurisy more times than any of us could remember. He did not go into the armed forces, but became an ARP man during the Second World War.

Because I can only remember back to the age of three my dear older sisters, Emmie, Matilda and Eileen, have written down some of their memories for me. They were quite an eye-opener.

My fifth eldest sister died in Australia in 1991, the same year as my beloved late husband, Fred. Queenie and her husband, Johnny, left their basement rooms with their first two children in Hackney, London, and travelled to Australia for a better life on the £10 Family Package, which it turned out to be after much hard work. They were called the £10 Poms. The fifth sister died before I could complete my family memoirs in a previous book.

Our mother had no miscarriages or abortions that we are aware of, but it cannot be ruled out because backstreet abortions with long sharpened knitting needles were a way of life in those days. There was no National Health Service until 1948 and it would be many many years before the Abortion Act was passed in Britain. To Mother's relief and ours in retrospect, there were no little Alberts!

You only have to look at pictures of the children of the depression years to observe at a glance the acute poverty. It was great men like Dr Barnardo and the philanthropist Lord Shaftesbury and other worthy ones, including of course William Booth of the Salvation Army, who set about trying to mitigate the plight of the poor.

Our mother's first seven daughters were born and lived in the tenement slums of Stepney and nearby. The last three were born in Essex. Some of us had two Christian names; some only one. I have no idea why. Mother could not remember either! She often got muddled up, calling out one name after another until she hit on the one she actually wanted! By that time we had all heard her hollering from streets away in Essex, and all gone running to her. She would say, "Oh! I only wanted [so and so] to run me an errand." What useful appendages our ears are!

Roughly speaking we were born with about two years between each of us, starting with Emmie in 1924. Mother fed us herself for as long as she could, which the working-class poor believed to be a crude form of birth control. It must have worked like a charm. There were no more babies for Mother after her tenth daughter.

Our mother, was a stickler for cleanliness and the term 'respectability' and practised what she preached. We were referred to as 'you girls' all our lives although our personalities were completely different.

We did have nicknames within the family. I was called Pansy Potter because I was well built and strong like the character in one of our weekly comics. Our Australian sister was Catsmeat because she kept an eye on the cat's-meat man's bicycle to make sure it wasn't pinched, and possibly sold! Eileen was called Whippet Quick because she was small and fast. None of us could recall why Emmie was nicknamed Pemshall. Matilda and Eileen were never taller than four feet eleven inches. When Matilda was born Granny said, "Oh, ain't she tiny!" From that day to her death Matilda was called Tiny by everyone, even at work.

Born into abject poverty as we most certainly were in London, somehow Mother managed to have 'best' dresses made for each of us using remnants from where one of her brothers worked. A sewing woman eking out her own poverty-stricken existence made the dresses for Mother's daughters and anyone else provided there were enough coppers or 'payment in kind'.

It was always the case that our mother made sure we were all dressed in the same colours – up until the girls left school, as a matter of fact. Easy for Mother to pick her girls out in a crowd. She was very proud to be seen out with her daughters en masse, just because they were all girls and born one after another with no boys at all. One can only imagine Father's disappointment at having no sons!

In London, work-wise the good times were very few and far between. The men took what jobs they could even if it was only for a few coppers.

The depression years hit the working class hard, nailing them to the ground. Not just in London either; also in America and other Western countries.

CHAPTER TWO

Our family moved to the Heathway in Dagenham, Essex, approximately 1938, after Queenie had rheumatic fever. How they managed that feat from the poverty of Stepney I do not know. Suffice it to say they were moved *by the powers that be* to a cul-de-sac road ever after called 'the Banjo' by Mother. She said, "I didn't like the Banjo – too many children with only one entrance to the road. The noise of them playing in the street was *murder*." (Dagenham Heathway.)

Somehow our family moved to a three-bedroomed house – rented albeit, in a better part of Dagenham. We always call it the six streets. One along with one at the bottom and four in separate lines. The one along was Fordyke Road. Leading off from it were Tenterden Road, Ross Avenue, Gerald Road and Winifred Road and at the bottom of those four going along Fordyke Road was Lamberhurst Road. It was modern and well built, with front and back gardens and an alleyway at the bottom of the back garden separating our houses from those in Ross Avenue. The landlord's rent collector lived in one of the houses in Fordyke Road.

The house, *48*, was in a small block of four houses: there was a very wide alleyway big enough for a car, but it was not then a car-owning society! There were blocks of houses and alleyways all along these roads.

By modern standards today the kitchen was minuscule and one of the three bedrooms was only a small box-room size, but having a bathroom, a back boiler to the fire and somewhere where they could breathe fresher air than Stepney was a godsend. They never moved from *48*. Mother brought her nine girls up in it. (Thelma died before they moved from Stepney.)

After the Second World War they bought *48* as sitting tenants and the girls' wages helped to pay the low mortgage, which we think was about £5 a month.

The house cost approximately £850 pounds. I cannot verify those figures.

The Second World War broke out in 1939. In 1940 when France capitulated to the Germans it was expected the Germans would then send an invasion force to conquer Great Britain. Another surge of evacuation of children to safer places was hurriedly set into motion.

I was still only four at this time when my sisters were to be evacuated with other children from the schools in Dagenham. London and other places expected to be heavily bombed. Because she'd had rheumatic fever Queenie was sent to a place in England not too far away.

Two sisters were to travel with their school to an *unknown destination*. Sitting on the bus with their classmates and their gas masks and bits and pieces, Eileen said, "Mother grabbed you, Vie, and sat you on my lap on the bus shouting out, *''Ere! Take Vilie or she might be killed!'''* Eileen grabbed my plump little body and held on grimly as the engine of the bus roared into life and gave a lurch forward. Quickly it sped off to the railway station taking its little occupants to an unknown destination and future. The mothers were screaming, sobbing and waving their sodden handkerchiefs, wondering if they would ever see their children again or when. Alas many children were blissfully unaware that they would become orphans, with their mothers killed by bombs and their fathers killed in action overseas.

Our mother gave birth to Doreen, her ninth daughter, in her bedroom at number *48* in 1940. She had already given birth to her eighth daughter at the Heathway, Essex, before they moved to *48* in Dagenham. Her tenth daughter was also born at *48* in 1942.

I don't think I would have had the courage of all the mothers of the evacuees. It must have been heart-rending! Having so many babies, Mother relied on the older girls to help her. The lives of the masses changed dramatically with full employment for those not in the services; there were regular wages and plain but wholesome hot meals in the canteens of the factories. They worked darned hard, especially in the production of aeroplane parts and tanks.

My husband, Fred, was taken out of mattress making after finishing his apprenticeship. Turned down grade 3 for the armed forces, he had to have a crash course in welding and as a welding fabricator. I think it may have been shorter than six months, being wartime. He then worked at Peckham Rye in London welding on war-work munitions and anything else needing welding. He lodged all over the place and worked round the clock in shift work until the end of the war in 1945.

I can *just* recall the rushing down to the air-raid shelters, the falling shrapnel and the fear. I cannot remember the bus, but I remember a little of when we arrived in South Wales and some of the train journey. We were dressed in our best – all I had was what I stood up in. It had not been *intended* that I would be evacuated. Children of my age were usually evacuated with their mothers. None of us were well off in 1940. True, we no longer lived in the slums of Stepney. Speaking for myself and my sisters, we were always spotlessly clean. Yes! We did wear a ragbag of hand-me-downs, but in Mother's eyes we were clean and *respectable-looking* – our mother's favourite phrase. In our social circles children scrubbed and cleanly dressed with good manners meant their parents were *somebody*. Mother always abided by *clean and respectable*, drumming it into us for evermore.

Thus on that evacuation day in England, the next chapter of my life began, *the Book of Life*. I still had *normal hearing*. I can distinctly recall the sounds of sobbing and screaming as young children were ushered on to the bus, then the train carrying us to an unknown destination – South Wales.

Some were in dirty raggedy clothing and had no luggage to speak of. All, however, had their gas mask on string over their chest, in plain cardboard boxes or with material covering them. What a motley assortment we must have presented to the good people of Wales. Yes, they did get a small payment for taking evacuees into their homes, but they did not know how long it would be for; neither did we! I can vividly remember being taken by the hand and walked up and down streets of Welsh houses. Up and down, up and down, knock knock. "Will you take an extra evacuee?" No, they would not! "She's too young – she should be with her own mam."

Memories are funny things – some you recall spot on, others elude you until you are an OAP. And then long-term memory comes to the fore, unexpectedly like flashes on the screen. I don't know who Eileen went to. Poor Eileen had an awful scar, from an accident with a poker when younger and it went the length of her cheek. We never notice it but others do and did. And, to cap it all, she was nearly of school leaving age – fourteen in those years.

After my severe illness in 1946 some memories elude me until suddenly they flash into my brain as clear as can be, so vivid. It is as if things had happened yesterday, instead of over half a century ago.

When my mother was alive and my wartime mam and dad too

they answered the questions I put to them to verify certain things or happenings in my life.

Alice, my Welsh mam, died in 1991 and Bill, my Welsh dad, in 1996.

Eileen was moved many times in 1940, then she went home to *48* to go out to work and earn a wage. My other sister went to the sister of my Welsh dad, Auntie Doll. Bill and Alice were living upstairs with Doll. Married in December 1939, they fell in love with me and I went to live in great happiness and contentment with my Welsh mam and dad until 1945. They had no children of their own until after the war. I was Alice's living doll, and she and Bill loved me to bits.

Today I suppose the politically correct would have refused Alice and Bill. They were living upstairs in one room and Alice was always overweight (by modern standards). However, this was wartime.

Back in London the children of the six streets had gazed in awe at all the men and boys (old enough) in their Royal Navy uniforms of navy blue, or their khaki army outfits or the lighter blue of the air force.

We had never seen them look so smart. Some, sadly, were never to be seen again. As the poet Rupert Brooke put it, 'There's some corner of a foreign field that is for ever England.' He never wrote a truer word. He could, however, have said the same about the Welsh and the Scots and the Irish. Millions of *corners of fields* that hold our men and women.

They hadn't wanted their young lives to be cut short so cruelly. War is always a young man's *game*! So it is said. Some game! Bravely they strode down the roads, kitbags hoisted on to broad shoulders, whistling jauntily, maybe almost scared to death but determined not to show it. They paused at the corners of their roads with one last cheery wave, then disappeared out of sight.

How many were too choked with emotion and afraid to say *goodbye*? A small word with a wealth of meaning. The softer term of *au revoir* was not generally in our vocabulary – not of the *real* working class. It saddens me even to think of it. Like the First World War conscripts, they had no choice.

Most evacuees and those who were not evacuated (of my generation) have never forgotten those times. We never will. It is our *awful heritage* to pass it on. As I tidy up this biography today in 2019 I am reminded of many of my neighbours who are now in their eighties who still have terrible memories of wartime. Their nightly dreams must be awesome and black at times. It is a measure of the indomitableness of the human spirit that the bad times are pushed back, and the happy times and camaraderie come to the fore. Thanks be to God.

After the Japanese bombed Pearl Harbor, America was well and truly into the war and the *friendly invasion* of the Americans into Great Britain came about. I have already spoken about this in my book *Sixteen Shillings and Tuppence Ha'penny* (Minerva Press, 2001; reprinted by Magna Large Print, 2003).

They were welcomed with open arms especially by the love-starved women and girls who had to dance together at the Palais dance halls. Lovely men, sadly many thousands, never again returned to their homeland and loved ones. Some are buried in the American Cemetery in England. There is a special room at the new Millennium Forum and Library in Norwich, Norfolk (2001), dedicated to the USAAF. You can read and see for yourself how many of the USAAF died, with spoken commentaries and rolls of honour and books about them. And at the cemetery in Cambridge it is a corner of America in an English field which is for ever *American. We owe them so much—*

During those bleak years 1939 to 1945 our families always had their ears glued to the radios at home or in the pubs. Alvar Lidell speaking in his distinctive voice gave us the latest news reports.

We had no televisions, only the radios, gramophones and newsreels at the cinema to show us how the war was progressing. We did have wonderful free-speech media in the newspapers that were cheap to buy. War correspondents and cameramen risked their own lives to be in the thick of the fighting to send news and pictures and films back to England and the rest of the *free* world. Many of them died too. They *also served.* We should never forget that fact. I never do.

At the cinema you could hear a pin drop from the audience, who sat mesmerised listening to the voice-over of the Gaumont and Pathé newsreels. Most of those watching and listening so intently had loved ones in the thick of the fray; it was absolutely terrifying for them to listen, let alone *watch*! But they did – had to – though many women and girls stumbled out into the night air blessing the darkness to hide their sobbing wet faces. *They also serve, those who stand and wait.* Letters were heavily censored. Often they just received a beige card with a tick by a brief printed message to say they were OK.

The war is well documented in many excellent books by people obviously more in the know than myself. All wars are terrible. Sadly the old adage rings true: *Those who desire peace should prepare for war.* And each man or boy killed was once upon a time some mother's beloved darling baby, smiling and gurgling happily.

Now it was 1940 and I was on the train to a *new country*! South Wales! Part of the British Isles, which include England, Scotland, Northern Ireland and Wales. Yes, our country used to include the whole of Ireland itself. Today, in 2019, we have England with no parliament of its own, devolution for Scotland with its own parliament, Wales with its assembly and Northern Ireland still going through its own process to government, and the television and other media call us the UK! Perhaps someday fairness will be given to England? In 1940 none of this would have entered our heads anyway. People of Great Britain, the Commonwealth and other places were all in the same boat: fighting the evil of Nazism.

On the train that day, little did I know it but my life was to be changed for ever, not just in Wales but when I returned to England in 1945. At the age of four I was far too young to think of the future.

I do remember that on return to my real family I had more than I departed with in the way of possessions! In 1940 I had just what I stood up in!

A brief thought just crossed my mind. In 1949 when I left the family home again for pastures new at thirteen years of age I possessed only what I stood up in!

CHAPTER THREE

Wales was very different from Stepney in London and *48* in Essex. The air smelt different. There were *slag heaps,* which we had never heard of. The Welshwomen held their babies a strange way, but it was a very comfortable way to do so. They had thick large shawls around themselves and the baby was neatly tucked into it, which was very wonderful and *mouth-opening* to us Londoners.

They spoke differently. *My ears* caught the sing-song soft lilt of the women's voices and I was captivated. Our motley assortment of evacuees was dumbstruck!

But there was *fear* amongst the motley assortment from England. Wales was a *foreign country* like Scotland and Ireland were. In those far-off days travel to other parts of Britain let alone abroad was unheard of in our poor societies. Several moaning Minnies set up ear-splitting caterwauling wanting their mums!

Some of the older streetwise urchins had the good old stiff British upper lip. Their mouths turned grimly inwards and downwards, desperately preventing themselves joining in the caterwauling. Even the cockiest of lads seemed to have accepted he had met his Nemesis! For a while! Hands in pockets, a few would-be *boyos* whistled softly, legs straight as a die, eyes darting hither and thither.

They *cased the joint*, so to speak. It must have been much harder for the older children than for myself. They knew what they had left behind, but didn't know how their lives would be now – a great staggering dilemma from their point of view. Me? So far I did have two of my sisters. We Humphreys *girls* were used to being looked after by the older sisters. It seemed just another outing with them. The train of course had been a bit of a puzzle, but no doubt it must have lulled me to sleep in Eileen's arms. 'Sufficient unto the day' is one of my mottoes.

On the way to Wales, children had palled up with others as they gradually acclimatised themselves to the journey. Some were former schoolmates, others were sworn enemies. The escorts were going to have their work cut out separating the *wheat from the chaff.* A mixture of assorted *allsorts* on that platform in 1940. Maybe that's why I recall it, though my sisters remembered too.

There are many books written about the evacuees by children who then were old enough to have better memories than myself.

That it was going to be, and was, a whole new *ball game,* to use an Americanism, was without a shadow of doubt. Nobody could foresee the length of the war, or if we would be invaded and *put under the jackboot.* It was a distinct possibility after the fall of France and the Dunkirk evacuation of our troops in 1940.

Yes, there are people who still have bad memories of their evacuation to Wales. But *my* memories of Wales are happy and carefree and cocooned in love. I am for ever grateful to the Welsh people, especially the Onions and Jenkins families, who all helped Alice to spoil her *living doll.*

One looks back in history to when we were warring factions, the English and the Welsh, and wonder what Owen and his ilk would think of the English *invasion* of the 1940s.

Well, Blackwood, now known as Gwent, South Wales, is in my eyes a precious *segment of my whole person.* Another chapter in the Book of Life.

I, pristine in new shiny shoes, dress and hair ribbon one fine Sunday was actually called a *dirty evacuee*! Did I hear that correctly? Of course. I was not deaf. And the person labelling me was as grimy an urchin as some of the motley assortment I travelled with. But this name caller was Welsh. It is the only time I can recall being accosted as such. I must have been about seven or eight years old then. "Dirty, dirty 'vac-oooee." Mortally wounded at an uncalled-for and wholly wrong slur I rushed to tell Alice. She was incandescent with rage that somebody was slandering her little *living doll.* Alice gave a few choice words to the scruff who'd accosted me. Plump and generously so, short of stature, my Welsh mam was quivering with rage. She folded me into her warm embrace: I was comforted and safe from all harm.

Alice and my Welsh foster-father, Bill, were my rock. They provided stability and happiness and comfort to a little English evacuee. After war broke out Alice and Bill married in December 1939 and had no children of their own. I was their *baby and pride and joy.* I came to think of Alice and Bill as my parents, my mam and dad!

I loved them and they and their relatives all loved me unconditionally. The Welsh working class was different to the English one. For a start, it was King Coal where I lived. Bill's hard graft, up to his armpits in damp and sometimes water, was digging out the coal. His wages helped to keep me and feed me. I have never forgotten that. We did not live in the slums of tenements as in London.

It was a big shock to older children.

In 1940 we knew nothing of Biros, washing machines, televisions, computers, word processors or mobile phones. Most people did not have cars, nor telephones in their houses. We did not have hovercraft, hover lawnmowers and thousands of other things taken for granted today. It was an entirely different world. We always referred to the *man in the moon looking down*. I could play freely out in the open without Mam worrying about anything happening to me – apart from grazing one's knees, of course. Simple things like that.

Back in England the children not evacuated played joyfully on the bomb sites, scavenging and jumping in and out of bomb craters, or counting bits of shrapnel or arranging swops with other children.

Being billeted in South Wales I probably didn't realise overly that there was a war on back home.

We never knew that someday man would land on the moon. We would have been laughed to scorn had we predicted it. *Life was not fanciful notions in 1940.* Earth was earth, the sky was the sky, the coal for the fire came from the coal mines.

Life was as we saw it around us in our daily lives. What we heard on the wireless or the films was the be all and end all of our existence.

It was a happy world for me in Wales, wonderfully, joyously happy and contented. What did it matter about non-existent long-range weather forecasts? We always took our cardigans and macs when we went anywhere. Common sense, wasn't it?

South Wales was a *gentle world* of people who clung to their roots and traditions and their chapels and singing.

Gentle, friendly sloping hills, lots of sky, no terribly high buildings, steep green valleys which seemed to *sing* in the crisp morning air. The slag heaps were not yet sky-high. Rows of little terraced houses with outside toilets hugged the sides of the valleys in some places.

My South Wales then appeared to be lovingly enfolded into the gentle arms of Mother Earth herself. Little hills, steep hills, valleys, daffodils, flocks of birds wheeling and dipping, circling us and swooping to be carried high aloft in the air currents. How green was *my* valley then – the land of song, streams, rivers and wildlife. My tubby legs flailing the air, I tumbled and rolled down the hills with my shrieks of joy and happiness and the rapture of the innocent. I could hear my playmates shrieking and shouting with me. *I was not deaf when I lived in South Wales*. Ah, memories of sound and chatter and camaraderie, and of Welsh singing.

I did not know the fear of falling bombs in Wales, or of falling shrapnel and incendiaries, or of the wet, dark claustrophobic air-raid shelters, of being wakened rudely from sleep and bundled by older sisters into old army blankets and rushed down to the shelter in the middle of the night, with the searchlights sweeping the dark skies of England, with its homes blacked out and no other lights to be seen because of blackout regulations forcibly adhered to. But I heard when I was in England. *I was not deaf then.* The ack-ack guns blasted away enough to shatter some people's sensitive eardrums. Tongue stuck to palate, cloying fear, wondering if we would survive the unknown night and enemy. These are my *earliest memories* before I went to stay in the Land of Song. It haunts me in my dreams sometimes. Some older children had more horrific memories than myself. Some had no idea of sleeping with sheets and pillowcases. And lice were rampant in their hair. The fleas never had it so good in those long-gone days of poverty. We all had them – adults too – in England.

Some children knew much more about what was happening. None could see the wood for the trees. Most of the Welsh people never left the valleys in their whole life from cradle to grave.

If I shut my eyes I can *picture my Wales* in the innocent years of 1940–45! On the whole the Welshwomen were like my mother, always washing and scrubbing and cleaning, eking out their men's hitherto pitiful coal-mining wages (increased in war years with *war effort*) to provide nourishment for their families, scrubbing or reddening front doorsteps, scrubbing the dirty clothes on the glass-and-wood washboards in the oval tin baths. The baths were used every night or morning according to the coal shifts, for their husbands to scrub clean their coal-begrimed bodies after their stints in back-breaking work in the bowels of the earth, providing house coal or steam coal. The women dashed in and out to the open fire ranges, keeping an eye on the cooking victuals, having a *breather* or a gossip at the front door in between if it was daytime.

With their men on shifts it was all go for the Welshwomen, raising the bairns, raising the evacuee children – some of the latter, sad to say, were *not very grateful*!

Mind you, they didn't *all* have loving foster-parents like my mam and dad, Alice and Bill Onions. I was extremely lucky and fortunate. Various scenarios spring to my mind. I can hear the women speaking in soft, gentle lilts (voices) to one another, "Ah! Bless their little hearts! D'you hear them cryin' for their mams, mon? Do make my heart bleed, it do!" (I've forgotten the spelling of some Welsh lingo.)

"Indeed to goodness! Aye, mon, it be taking some getting used to, will it now? 'Specially them from the towns. But then – dinna fach, mon! Little ones forget quite quickly, y'know! Aye, mon, they do!"

"Aye, well, dinna fach yourself, mon, I know y'know, but well, Mrs Jones – ah well, dinna fach, says I."

Beautiful nostalgia for a gentle way of life now long gone. Mists of time blur the edges and my soft Welsh world is with me again. How lucky we were to live then – war or no war!

I find myself lucky once again to live in another gentle world: in a small market town in England where courtesy reigns in the shops and around me. I'm privileged to live amongst former city folk who were the men and women of 1939–45 – the heroes and heroines who saved us from the Darkness of Evil, the people who kept sanity in our homeland and watched and waited for loved ones fighting on foreign soil or on the sea or in the skies – servicemen and women of all ranks, and civilians who all played their part so we could be a free country with our own free Parliament and laws, *our own coinage and our sovereignty, which have served us well for thousands of years.* I pray we never relinquish any of it and betray those who died for our freedom and rights to rule ourselves our own justifiable way.

I live amongst people who survived the horrors of the Holocaust or the tortures of the Far East prisons and evacuees who lost their whole families to war. To live amongst such people now in this gentle town is an honour and a privilege.

It makes me feel humble, yet uplifted, to know there are still gentle places to live in England amongst such good folk as I was privileged to live amongst, like the gentle Welsh folk.

I often thank God for the Welsh, who were so good to us evacuees. I humbly pray that they and those I now live amongst all live their remaining years in peace, happiness and comfort. They *served their time*!

Nostalgia is a powerful life force. These are times of drug-ridden, crime-polluted towns and cities; despite the terrible horrors of the war years we were very fortunate to live *then*!

We had community spirit and real communities; the extended family was the norm, just as it was in my happy Welsh valleys.

CHAPTER FOUR

Alice and William Onions (known as Bill) lived at 1 Rock Cottages, next to The Rock Inn Public House, just outside Blackwood and on the main road to Tredegar and Markham. Today the cottage is part of The Rock Inn. It was from 1940 onwards owned by Mrs Esau (she ran it, but she could have been the manager). The buses stopped outside our front door and there was no frontage to the cottage. The front door opened on to the road. Further up the main road there were the coal-miners' cottages. Oakdale and its large pit could be seen over the valley from the front bedroom window of our cottage.

Up the Rock Hill at the side of our cottage the very steep hill led to the Rock Chapel, the Calvinistic Methodist church, which had been opened in 1839 by the efforts of Evan Jones.

The Rock Chapel was enormously part and parcel of our lives. It gave me a good grounding in faith. I remain truly grateful for that reason. It has been part of my foundation and remains with me to this day. And the singing! Ahhh! I was not deaf when I lived in South Wales. I don't think a choir of Welshmen singing can be beaten. It enters into your ears and remains for ever.

Today we have popular singers from Wales in the persons of Bryn Terfel, Tom Jones, Aled Jones and Charlotte Church – internationally known songbirds. When they are on television I put a new battery into my body-worn hearing aid and turn the television sound on full blast. And I rejoice and thank God that I can *hear* the *beat* of the music and their voices.

Many of the scales of the music I cannot *catch* at all. Likewise on *The Last Night of the Proms*, shown on television, I do the same. At the end of the programme I shut my eyes, bow my head and quietly thank the Lord God and I ask Him to let me be able to *catch the beat* of next year's performance! (I can never pick up the sound of the beginning of 'The Blue Danube' with my powerful hearing aid. I can get the *beat* of low sounds best of all.)

I digress. Bill sent me a book not long before he died about Blackwood, and I read there about Evan Jones, who was so central to the building of the chapel. Apparently he was from Llangeitho, Cardiganshire, and he was a master at the Bedwellty School, Blackwood.

My Welsh mam, Alice, wrote to me faithfully until her death. Then Bill, my Welsh dad, took over the letter writing just as faithfully until his death in his early eighties. Every birthday and Christmas the first cards were sent by Alice; after her death my Bill carried on the *tradition*. This is one of the letters from Bill.

21st October 1992

Dear Vie,

So glad you enjoyed the photos of you when you were young. It is great to look back on life but I have not come across one of the three of us together. Alice kept so much of you. She still had the box you sent your wedding cake in. Cuttings from the newspapers about you passing your exams to the Grammar School. The Winston Churchill Award and a few others. I love to go to the Rock Chapel where Mam and Dad took us from the time we were born. [Bill's parents, Gran and Grandad, the Rock.] It is like going home there [the Rock Chapel]. There are not many Sundays I miss. [Bill now lived in the town of Blackwood and took a taxi to and from the chapel on Sundays in his old age.] There is a feeling of peace there and Alice always believed that. We are very few in numbers now; as the old pass away [die] we have no young ones coming in. Only about sixteen members left now. [It used to be packed solid when I lived in Wales.] So we have to fight to keep it open. The hymns you ask for are sung very often and when they are sung I can always see.

Someone who has passed away, everyone has a favourite. Ethel [Bill's sister] and Harold from Newport has [sic] just come to visit me as she never misses. Always it is a cake or a pastry. Rene [Bill's other sister] seldom comes as she has been ill with her nerves. She is lucky she has four boys and a few grandchildren. Three of them have been divorced and married again. Have not been very well myself for a fortnight. Doctor thinks it may be that now the 'shock' has hit me! He said that for two years I [Bill] did everything for her [Alice] and now I miss it all. Thank you for the photo of your grandson. [He meant my granddaughter Charlotte.] She has your smile. God has been good to you with so many blessings life has changed a lot in this day and age. We could go to the pictures [cinema] in Blackwood three old pence [travel] and one penny to go in, one for chips and one for sundries. You could go to Newport on the train for one old shilling and sixpence [7½p.]. Now if we had any trains it would be a few pounds. I know when my poor Alice was in hospital the taxi fare was ten pounds each way. Never mind we must be grateful when we see the suffering that is going on in this world.

God bless you,
Bill.

Apart from correspondence I do not know what Alice and Bill were like in their last years. A former teacher of mine at my London school for the deaf once said (when she was very old and still corresponding with me) that she had a friend who was a nun. This nun told her that sometimes it is better to remember old friends as they *were* in our happy memories of yesteryear. But I did go back, on my own as a *teenager* and again with my husband and two sons. I was often in poor health and it was better for them to keep me in their memories as I did them. They were and always will be in my heart, my Welsh mam and dad.

The Rock Chapel was Presbyterian in Bill's last years. Such stories it could tell if it could talk, of the coal miners and their lives: births, marriages and funerals, prayers for those involved in pit accidents and so on. The coal mine which Bill worked in during 1940–45 was small with no pit baths. It was the Primrose Coal Mine – a pretty name for the black treasure from it. What tales that mine could tell if it could talk!

Today when I browse through my *Country Life* magazines I compare the photos in it to the *memories* of Wales as I knew it in the war years. It is sad to see in England churches which have become *redundant* (due partly to moving populations) and turned into houses. But I am sure that Jesus would have approved for He said everyone had their *home* except the Son of Man. There must be lots of love in those redundant places. Like Bill's heart, mine keeps a corner for the Rock Chapel.

Because of the horror of the Blitz, our mother and her toddler number eight and also baby Doreen turned up at the Jenkins and Onions homes for a few weeks. Our mother took Eileen back with her, to go to work and fetch home wages – sorely needed. There was no family allowance then. The other sister was not happy and was very miserable. She went back to England. It would be another pair of hands with the babies.

I remained with my Welsh mam and dad and I never saw my English family again until 1945, at end of the war in Europe. Our mother had no telephone and neither did my mam.

Where they all slept those few weeks in the Jenkins and Onions homes I do not recollect. It's sufficient to say it was boundless hospitality from Welsh families. My mother and sisters always spoke highly of the Welsh people, especially the Jenkins and Onions families.

Eileen would be fourteen the following March and the other sister did not fit in, so home she went too. According to Bill I was a *loveable, laughing little girl with always a beautiful smile.*

Jack Perry has a wonderful memory of the old days, and still lives but a few miles from his old home of our childhood years. His wife, Betty, an expert typist, writes his dictated letters to me and they bring Wales vividly back to life.

The railway tracks for the coal trucks ran across the top of the tunnel. As children, Jack, Ronnie, Alan, Donald, Margaret, Betty, Maisie and I, and lots of others at the Villas, played on the railway tracks and *built hideaways* with some of the wood at the sidings. Later on, when Maureen was billeted with me and my foster-family she joined us. Maureen's father was a soldier billeted nearby, probably at Maesrudded Mansion. Her mother came to visit him.

Close by under the tunnel were lots of tiny terraced cottages. I recollect the size of them and the darkness within. Gran and Grandad (the Rock), Bill's parents, lived in one of them. The cottages appeared to literally hug the sides of the valley, to the best of my memory. Gran and Grandad Onions came to our cottage mostly en route to and from the services at the Rock Chapel. They were very devout Christians and faithful to the Rock Chapel. (It is today permanently closed – so sad.)

June 10th 1967

Dear Mr and Mrs Foot [Grandad was always polite],
   We were so pleased to hear from you, it did really cheer us up in our illness to think that you still remembered us after so long a time. [He meant me still keeping in touch since 1945.] We are still not able to go out to chapel, the place where we long to be to give thanks for all God's Mercy to us in the past and to give us faith to Trust Him for the Future. I was pleased to hear you loved our singing in the Services and you loved been [sic] amongst us hear [sic]. It was a Pleasure to Know you.
   Times have changed, you were Violet to us. Now you are married and got a family. May God Bless You All. And may you train them to lead a good Christian Life. To enjoy Health and Happiness, for the Rest of Your Life.
   Love from Gran and Grandad THE ROCK. Thank you for your memories.
   Till we meet again, all the best.

I keep this letter pasted inside my confirmation book. Each time I went into hospital (I have been many, many times) I read this letter, shut my eyes, and was transported to the Rock Chapel and its warm loving interior, giving me strength and peace. It's been in my handbag now since 1967!

It was Granma and Pop Jenkins up at Cefn Fforest who spoilt

me. To them I *was* their granddaughter! They didn't have much, but what they had they shared.

Many years into the future Alice and Bill left our cottage and became caretakers at the Rock Chapel. But not before I had managed to get my husband and two sons and a van full of deaf children (en route back to London we did a detour specially for me!) to see them unexpectedly after a few days on the Gower Peninsula and the Pendine Sands with Dennis Uttley, a teacher of the deaf, as the driver! And we met their grown-up son, Colin, for the first time, and their dog – a surprise which Bill and Alice took in their stride, inviting us into the tiny two-up two-down cottage and stuffing us full of freshly made sandwiches!

In 1940 at 1 The Rock, Alice had an old-fashioned black kitchen range. Summer and winter there was a cheerful fire going. The hot water for Bill's daily bath was heated in a bucket on the range. We had no electricity in our cottage. The wireless (radio) ran on accumulators which had to be *seen to* (topped up) every so often. There was a gas mantle hanging from the middle of the ceiling by two chains.

I don't remember if we had gas upstairs; I think we used night lights in a saucer of water!

The front room downstairs was only used to go through to the front door for the fresh milk from the large gleaming milk churns of Hywell-the-Milk. Hywell Jones is a first cousin of Betty Perry (their fathers were brothers). Hywell-the-Milk kept his pristine long-handled ladles hanging over the sides of the churns. Carefully he ladled the creamy milk into our fat blue jug. With my chubby hands holding the jug and with bated breath I edged back inside our front door, careful not to spill a drop, to prove I was *old enough* to carry the milk! I'd feel awfully chuffed when Alice beamed and chuckled saying, "Indeed to goodness."

Number 1 was next door to The Rock Inn and there was a cottage the other side, to the best of my memory. It is now one long pub, called The Rock Inn, just outside the town of Blackwood.

Near the small town of Blackwood was Meredith-the-Blacksmith. He was a fine man, a gentleman. I loved to go and see him. He would blow on his thumb and his biceps swelled! I thought he was awfully clever and strong!

Jack Perry remembers him too. When Jack married he and his wife bought their first home next door to where Meredith lived between the Rock and Blackwood (Cwmgelli).

Incidentally Jack was telling me that Maesrudded is now the Maes Manor Hotel and that the two cinemas have closed – one

24

demolished, one converted into a bingo hall. Blackwood used to be all National Coal Board housing or council housing, but there have been many changes with new homes built since the war.

A number of the chapels in Blackwood have closed, but they still have a Baptist church, a Methodist church and the Presbyterian church at The Rock and the old parish church of Bedwellty.

I reckon in 1940–45 I must have been one of the most loved and happy evacuees in South Wales!

Just before he died, Bill said they took me out for the day one Sunday and on the way back through Blackwood looking in the shop windows I spied a doll of some sorts – celluloid possibly? Bill tried to pacify me by saying the shop closed on Sundays so he couldn't buy it for me. I kicked up a *stink* and he had to carry me all the way home – crying. "And *that* was the only time we ever had any trouble from you!"

At number 1, Rock Cottage, there were two downstairs rooms and two upstairs. No bathroom! We ate, washed, bathed and lived our daily life in the kitchen. The toilet was outside in the handkerchief-sized yard. The garden where Alice hung the washing was an overgrown place at the side of the Rock Hill. Alice was ever plump and cuddly, but she should have been as thin as a lath with walking up and down the Rock Hill to chapel and to hang out the washing and bring it back in. The steep staircase in the little cottage went straight up to a tiny landing in the form of a stairwell with two doors, one on either side of it. My mam and dad's room was at the front and mine was at the back, with the outside stone staircase from the yard and its gate almost on a level with my bedroom window, which became their son Colin's when he was born after the Second World War.

The kitchen, as were all kitchens at that time, was the everyday room. The kitchen table was in the centre. The kitchen sink was where Alice bathed me regularly when I was very young until I *graduated* to the little tin bath – the very one Bill used for his daily bath, for he got really black from the coal mine. There were no pit baths at the Primrose mine.

At the kitchen table, which was scrubbed cleaner than clean every day, we ate our meals. I did all my little childish drawings and paintings sitting at it.

Our mother and my Welsh mam had something very much in common: *cleanliness is next to godliness.*

In most homes in the forties, before the age of mass-market television sets, there was always a large table in the centre of the room which everyone actually lived in each day. In England it was called the *living room*. I presume that applied elsewhere in the British Isles too, but I don't actually know.

Of course we had no television – never heard of them. We did have the *precious* accumulator radio, *filled up* or *topped up* periodically as the house ran on gas.

On the old black coal-fired kitchen range Alice made lip-smacking rice puddings with their tops sprinkled with nutmeg.

For large coal-mining families with more than one man or boy (teenager) working the mines in shifts, the bathing ritual entailed the hard graft of filling buckets and hoisting them on to the open coal fires. One good thing was they were never short of coal in our cottage.

If it was still light when Bill's shift ended Alice told me to sit on the doorstep out front and wait for him. The front door was kept ajar so she could keep an eye on me. She knew I would not run in front of the buses or the occasional horse and cart. I was sensible. Traffic of the combustion-engine kind was not jam-packed on the road running past our cottage. It was wartime. I cannot ever recall travelling in a private car until I returned to England, and that was only the car of Cissie Mills' father, who lived in Lamberhurst Road near *48*. I had been in ambulances in England and went in the *school minibus* when I went to West Ham School for the Deaf in London, 1947–49.

Sitting on the doorstep I eagerly waited for my dad. Bill and his mates hove into view with string tied round their knees (just below) – to keep the rats from going up his trousers, Bill always said!

Their kind begrimed faces black with coal dust used to break into huge grins, their teeth sparkling white. Some whistled cheerily. It must have been a relief to come up from that *black hell*. For me it was one of the highlights of my life. Until I returned to England I was under the naive impression that all families included men who were coal miners, apart from families of shopkeepers, teachers, priests and the milk delivery man.

When I did return to England, the land of my birth, it was quite a culture shock to find families with not one coal miner and there were no coal mines near *48*.

My Welsh miners slaked their thirst at The Rock Inn. It was brought out to them in their regular pint pot. They'd sup, cough and with twinkling eyes say to me, still sitting patiently on the doorstep, "*How be Violet, mon?*"

I was dead chuffed. My little heart swelled with pride and I said, "*Very well, thank you, mon,*" and they'd chuckle a bit. I was so proud of my coal miners. Proud to see them arrive and proud to see them trudging back to their own homes on Shanks's pony (walking). Wet or dry, the Welsh walked everywhere, or so it seemed. Sturdy of build, they had strong legs and rippling muscles. You couldn't have finer friends than *my* coal miners.

On the wall in the cottage's front parlour there was a large photo of Alice and her beautiful sister Esther. I would have liked that old-fashioned photo as a memento.

In wintertime I went sleighing (tobogganing) with the children from the terraces and other homes further up from The Rock. Over the road opposite the cottage we lived in was a tunnel and the trucks carrying coal passed over on railway lines. There was a steep hill to Grandad the Rock's cottage. The hill went past it, and when it was covered in snow we had enormous fun sliding down on our toboggans. Mine was a good one made by Bill with the metal runners made by Meredith-the-Blacksmith.

When I was very young Bill always sat on the toboggan with me. Later as I grew older I was allowed to go down by myself. Oh! Utter bliss! I couldn't think of anything more delightful than to whizz down the hillside and end up in the piled-up snowdrifts at the bottom with shrieks and the cheers of my mates ringing in my ears.

A few years ago the *Daily Mail* had my photo on their letters page and Jack Perry, an old playmate, sent me a long letter, which was a wonderful surprise. The postmen here were very good – they found me with just my name and the area and county, which was under the newspaper photo. That very day I had been looking through the original papers of my autobiography and was thinking of the sleighing. It is amazing that Jack Perry also referred to the sleighing. His dear wife Betty types his letters and it has given a wonderful fillip to my life to be able to share those long ago memories again.

Jack Perry and Betty have filled me in about a few things. They still live not far from The Rock and Jack's old home. I did not recall that Hywell-the-Milk was related to them. That was pleasant news. I am able to incorporate some of Jack and Betty's memories from their letters. I am very grateful.

In recent years I have read of some former evacuees having dreadful billeting experiences during 1940–45, but all my memories are honestly and emphatically golden ones of Mam, Dad, their relatives and my mates. I loved the Welsh people and I always shall.

Just think! If I had not gone to live back in England I would have normal hearing now! But then again, I might not have had such a vast enriching experience of life as I have in many ways and directions. I guess the good Lord looked after me. He gave me the best mam and dad He had in Wales!

Our parents and my sisters all talk affectionately of how well looked after I was and of my Welsh mam and dad. They always told people about that fact. They could not say enough about the goodness of the Jenkins and Onions families. In the Holy Christian Bible Jesus talks about taking strangers into one's home. My mam and dad took that literally and loved a stranger 100 per cent.

Here in Downham Market, Norfolk, I often light candles for my Welsh parents, Alice and Bill Onions. When I rise from my knees (with difficulty nowadays!) I smile warmly as I picture their loving faces and hear their soft lilting voices in my head. "Dinna fach, Violet, mon."

After the war when Colin arrived on the scene he went to grammar school in Wales and I in England, yet none of my English siblings had higher education in any form. I do not say that in any way detrimental to my sisters; it's just that both Colin (after the war) and myself, raised by Alice and Bill – we both made grammar school. What a coincidence!

At Rock Cottages during part of the war Maureen was billeted with us at Rock Cottage. Her mother was very nervous. Her husband was in the armed forces. We all liked her. She was a generous soul who shared what she had. Alice teased her for *shovelling* the powder on to her face. It was nothing nasty and she took it in good spirit. I loved her. Whatever she bought and brought down for Maureen she did the same for me.

The last time my Welsh parents heard from Maureen was when she'd had a heart attack, and then they heard no more. According to Bill, in a letter to me a few years back, he'd lost all trace of her. I forgot to ask her married name. He said she had married and had a family.

One Christmas morning Maureen and myself woke early and looked at the hitherto empty fireplace in our bedroom. Lo and behold! There was a blackboard and easel each. In our stockings we each had a *china*-faced cloth doll and other gifts. We each had the same gifts. Plump little Violet and slimmer little Maureen got on like a house on fire. I cannot recall the dates Maureen lived with us at the cottage and I forgot to ask Bill before he died. Mindful of wartime posters and instructions of *Careless Talk Costs Lives,* I did not query (I was a child) where her father was – if he was a soldier or an officer. I was just told her father was "in a big house nearby". Jack Perry and I think it must have been at the big hall. Love and God bless if you are still alive, Maureen.

Her mother always looked smart and well groomed in 1939–45, as if to say to old Adolf, "You won't break us!" She and my English siblings of the older generation were contemptuous of old Hitler, and in spite of dire shortfalls of just about everything in the way of cosmetics, toothpastes, stockings and clothing they held their heads proudly. They improvised with *make do and mend* and borrowed or scavenged whatever they could. It was important not to let the *ruddy Hun* think he had broken *their spirits and resolve*. One cannot but look back and admire the adults and *teenage* people of the war years. Their spirit was indomitable with it. In high heels, with her scarlet-slash mouth of a ruby-red lipstick and her *white* powdered face, she was quite a contrast to Alice, who was a homely little woman, short and plump. To go to school in Blackwood, Maureen wore a sort of navy or black velour coat, top quality! A similar coat, but more like a Burberry raincoat, was obtained for me. Whether that was from her I do not know. I would not have been surprised if it was. She was a generous soul. She even wore silk stockings! Where she got them from I have no idea. Nobody else we knew had them. They had disappeared at the outbreak of war.

My older sisters in England were still wearing gravy browning on their legs with a seam drawn up with a black pencil – except my sister Emmie, whose boyfriend was an American GI – even after VJ day, 1945!

Maureen and I were always two of the best dressed girls around, the smartest of smartest evacuees. I was *still* Alice's *living doll*, before Cliff Richard's song.

To visit relatives over at Oakdale, Alice and Bill walked us for miles! In the front garden there was a huge tree or shrub which was covered with masses of clusters of white flowers. I childishly termed it *my snowball tree over at Oakdale*. Alice was wearing her second-best hat on a picnic near the river with me and Maureen. It was, at first, a gorgeous day. We paddled safely in a little pool by some rocks. Suddenly the sky darkened deeply, and the rain came in sheets – literally! *When it rains in Wales there are no half measures* – we were soaked soggy. Alice bitterly snatched her sodden *second-best* hat from her head and threw it as far as her fat arms let her! She was so mad at the rain spoiling our picnic and her hat. The funny side got the better of her and she laughed out loud, twirling around like Julie Andrews in *The Sound of Music*!

We couldn't believe it was Alice's hat actually flying through the air! She must have been feeling *awfully mad* because one did *not* throw away *anything* in the war years! We were the *make-do-and-mend* generation!

For Sunday tea we went up to Cefn Fforest to Granma and Pop Jenkins, with their other children, like Philip and Nipper and Esther, and seemingly half of South Wales in and out of the house. A proper *railway-terminus* lot! Front and back doors were always unlocked and open; nobody was turned away. Alice's brother was courting a beautiful lass and his trousers were about three sizes too big for him in length and width. He wore them bunched round his waist with a thick brown wide leather belt. The men used to tease him.

He took it in good part and grinned broadly. The poor girl blushed fiery red and rushed out of the house. Pop laughed and told the men, *"Leave be, mon – you were courtin' once!"* On cue he hitched his belt and trousers a bit higher and dashed after his lady love.

Many Welsh words were bandied which meant nothing to my innocent ears, but seemingly there were some saucy and naughty epithets!

The Jenkins and Onions families treated me as their own. I was plump and pretty and always smiling and a great favourite long before Maureen came (they treated me the same after she came too). A veritable plump little pudding, they'd toss me in the air and fuss over me as if I was a precious jewel!

Philip was Alice's youngest brother and he was delegated to keep an eye on me up at Cefn Fforest when I went into the street. A kindly courteous man, Pop Jenkins would threaten Philip with his buckled belt if anything happened to me! Poor old Philip. He is married now with his own family in Herefordshire.

Our long walks took us for miles, often through the graveyards of churches. My memory is of happy smiling faces and the deep voices of the men and the lilting sing-song voices of the women tinkling in my ears. *Precious sound is mine to keep in my book of memories – in my head.* It could have been Bedwellty Church where I saw the most growing daffodils, but it could have been another place. At Easter I always think of those walks with the daffodils and Wordsworth's poem slips easily through my mind and I am transported back to 1940–45. Amid the horror of war and the futility of the killing the beauty of the daffodils comes to my mind. I can never see daffodils without remembering those lovely Welsh walks. In those carefree days of my childhood wild flora and fauna abounded – greenery as far as the eye could see.

So many people to wish *bora da* to or *nos da*. The walks to church, the walks to chapel, the walks to school, to *relatives* – ahh! How fortunate we are to have our memories of sights and sounds, walks for walking's sake, walks across the valley! We had strong legs!

Sitting on a mountainside for Alice to catch her breath, Bill would pluck certain ferns and grasses and twist them together like little Christmas trees.

Bill would tell me about something or other which was growing and I'd turn to Alice and say, "Mam, is that true?"

Alice replied, "If your dad says it's true, then it is mon, dinna fach!"

A thick branch grew from a certain tree on a bankside in the woodland where we went collecting hazelnuts, not far from home. Bill tied a rope to the branch with a loop at the end and twisted a smaller branch through it. Taking turns, we children *sat* with our legs on the branch on either side of the rope. With a running jump we sailed off the bank to whoops of joy and merriment for hours on end. Pure innocence!

The *playmates* from the Villas and other homes at bottom of the Tredegar Valley often joined in, and one of my most enduring memories is that run down the bank and sailing through the air on the *swing*.

Spring, summer, autumn, winter – the seasons of Wales were memorable in my childhood days.

Philip, Maureen, myself and the playmates went blackberrying. You've never seen such plump, succulent, juicy *black black*berries! We were all stained round our mouths, of course, by the time we got home with our string-handled jam jars. Bill made them for us so we could carry them more safely. Alice made blackberry pies – one for us and one for each of the grandparents. Much *oohhhing and ahhhhing* when we took them to Cefn Fforest for Sunday tea and down to the Onions down at The Rock.

Esther (Hetty) got married to Wilf, a sailor in the Royal Navy. I was very young and so was Winnie – we were bridesmaids. The photo (see page 73) is in black and white; we actually wore pale-green pink-rosebud-sprigged long dresses with matching hats (bonnets) held out in front with hidden wire. The only time I've ever been a bridesmaid!

Esther was a picture in white satin – she really was a beauty. I wonder where the material came from in wartime? Esther was *knock-down gorgeous* in ruched satin and Wilf was in his matelot gear. A real picture! I don't know if he was injured by an escaping German prisoner or if he was killed in the wartime sinkings or what? I was too young! And I have never thought to ask.

Alice and Bill did once send me a photo of Winnie in the eighties dancing at their social club in Blackwood. We must be similar ages, but I would not have known her from the shy little girl at the wedding of Wilf and Esther.

In my teens I went back to Wales and Bill took me to see Esther, who had happily remarried. Her youngest child toddled in sans nappy, making Bill laugh and say, "Where's yer trousers, mon?"

How green was my valley in Wales!

CHAPTER FIVE

Wonderful, glorious, May 1945! The war was over. Good had triumphed over the evil of Nazism. The house painter Schicklgruber, alias Hitler, was dead in his bunker: suicide with his blonde girlfriend, Eva Braun. Hurrah! The world could breathe freely again – but not yet in the Far East, where our *forgotten* boys were still fighting the Japanese! First things first. Europe was free! No more concentration camps, which knowledge shown on our cinema-screen newsreels shook us to the core. How could men be so evil! Horrendous!

Trafalgar Square was packed solid. My dearest late husband of thirty-six years' happy marriage was older than me and he was working as a welder on war work in Peckham Rye. Until his last years he couldn't recall *where he went* or *who with* for three whole days of celebration! He said strangers were hugging and kissing one another, dancing almost non-stop *around the clock* in Trafalgar Square. Their adrenaline kept them going when their body clocks should have given up.

There was no nastiness; it was all joy, joy, joy! He said the feeling of relief that it *was all over* was practically exquisitely unbearable. "And no more fire watching on the roofs of the firm at night!" No more working round the clock in shifts, lucky to snatch a few hours' sleep in between the air-raid warnings and the all-clear, playing cards and smoking like chimneys just to keep awake in between shifts! No more lodgings bombed and having to find new ones! A future to look forward to at last!

Fred had a faraway look in his eyes as he told me, as if he was living it all over again! Because of his deafness Fred was turned down grade 3. He'd tried hard to join his brother Arthur's regiment. He said it was terrible going into a pub not in uniform. He got dirty looks from the servicemen. But they that did the war work at home also served! Without their efforts how would the war have been won? The factory workers were magnificent. They faced mortal danger day and night with very little sleep for six years. Fred was in the thick of the Blitz when 40,000 houses a week got hit badly, 1,000 people a night killed in London.

My Fred said that one night the fires were so bad everybody thought the whole of London was alight. Like Dante's *Inferno,* he described it. He said he'd never been so frightened in all his life as he was that night, doing his bit on the factory roof – fire-watching, putting out incendiaries with sand. There were twenty-eight fires on St Paul's, and eight of Wren's churches were destroyed. Horrifying numbers of firemen were killed and injured. I wonder how many of the children who hadn't stayed evacuated in 1940, but returned home, were killed that night? In June 1940 there were some 100,000 evacuated on 180 trains. More followed – in July 4,000 – but many of them were back by the early winter months!

They also served who stood and waited! They made the aeroplanes and ammunition and petrol tanks and the big tanks and everything else necessary for the war effort. Women worked as they had never worked before! For each pilot in the sky there were umpteen ground crew to get them there! *Lest we forget,* civilians were as brave as many serving men and women. The ordinary people were our rock. They kept the homes going even if they were bombed out! They provided the sanity and love for our fighting servicemen and women to come home to. They were stalwart in the face of continual day-and-night bombing and its attendant privations. Alas, for many who hopefully waited there were no happy reunions! Grief was piled upon grief, but they swallowed hard and put on their best faces to join the celebration of the war being over.

I was now nine and a half years old. The England I had left as a toddler of four was now welcoming back the young schoolgirl, albeit a very Welsh one!

The Pathé and Gaumont newsreels at the cinema showed us the celebrations in England, especially in London, the crowds doing the Conga, the Lambeth Walk, and the hokey-cokey round the fountains in Trafalgar Square. London looked like one huge birthday party. Strangers were handing out fags and drinks as if there was no tomorrow, as if they had become millionaires overnight! An illusion, the latter – but who cared?

"London could take it," they said – and it did. They proved it with their high-spirited revels. Even in the cinemas people were shouting, whistling and cheering themselves hoarse at the scenes on the newsreels. Infectious joy! The hateful dangerous blackout was gone. Lights streamed everywhere. The whole of London was lit up like one huge bulb! Such lighting had not been seen for six long, dark, evil years. Praise be to God for the lights of victory! Windows, shops, doorways – everywhere it was "Let there be light." Never was light so heartily celebrated! Church bells tolled with hearty loud abandon from one end of our island to the other. Nobody worried about headaches; now it was joyful, thankful celebration. Those inside the churches knelt in humble gratitude to the Almighty for saving our island and its people from the dreaded horror of the evil jackboot. Candles were lit for those who died.

The Royal Princesses, Elizabeth, who had served in a regiment, and Margaret, were granted permission by their father, His Majesty George VI, to go *outside* Buckingham Palace *on foot* and mingle with the joyful yet happily respectful crowds as their parents waved from the balcony! In South Wales near our cottage we had a huge bonfire on the mountainside and woodland, and the last part still burning at the end was an old oil drum. Tables were laid out the length of roads for party food, and the memory of 'We'll Keep a Welcome in the Hillside', sung with gusto as only the Welsh can, will remain with me to my dying day.

And I?

Well! It was time for me to say goodbye to my beloved Welsh foster-parents, who had raised and guided me from four to nine and a half years of age. It was painful and heartbreaking and the actual parting is blocked out of my brain! It hurt so much!

Bill, overcome himself, thought Alice would die from grief (they had no children). I was her dear little *baby*!

The Jenkins and Onions families were grief-stricken, but I had to go – Mother wanted her seventh daughter back even though Bill and Alice had asked to adopt me. I had to go! My own heart was shattered! I barely remembered my family in England. I was Welsh now!

No longer would I hear the memorable singing of the Welsh voices at the Rock Chapel, singing *Cwm Rhondda* ('Guide Me O Thou Great Redeemer'), no longer would I chat to the blue-stubbled coal miners outside The Rock Inn.

My Welsh world! It was all over. For ever!

CHAPTER SIX

It was 1945 and in London the red double-decker bus wound its way through the bombed rubble on either side of the roads; skeleton buildings hung skew-whiff with torn wallpaper hanging dolefully in ragged strips. It seemed almost sacrilege to ogle what had once been people's homes! We children could only silently observe, not saying anything because we didn't know what to say or what was going to *actually* happen to us. I can remember we went to some kind of hall and sat at long trestle tables and were given corned beef, some cold potatoes and jelly! Dear war-torn England's hasty *welcome home* to its *long-lost* children soon to be returned to family or relatives or orphanages or whatever!

The forlorn buildings played on my mind. I'd not got the *nous* to understand the heartache and sorrow they epitomised, to understand the reality and fear and terror which England had (especially its cities) faced up to and conquered. Wales had sheltered me from the reality of war.

Suddenly, without preamble, Wales seemed a million light years away and my roots took hold *automatically* once again.

Word flew like wildfire: "The evacuees are back!" We waved bemusedly to people (from our bus) who were waving frantically and blowing kisses. How strange! We blew kisses back to them, laughing ourselves silly in the rush of excitement at this England of our yesteryears. Exactly what we were *doing* and *why* was neither here nor there. We just felt a common euphoria. Of course war had been seen on the newsreels, but as I'd been cocooned in Wales England was a new *land* to me in my tender years. The reality of the bombing only hit myself and many others on that bus, as we went past bombed building after bombed building, seeing the huge craters where there had been direct hits. After my life-threatening illness in 1946 some of my memories have been obliterated, but I do remember going en masse into the huge hall, sitting at long trestle tables to *eat* the welcome-home feast.

In Wales I had the best Alice could get for me in the way of clothing and shoes. A local *dressmaker* eking out an existence herself made my dresses. I wore patent leather (or something similar) for shoes. They were very shiny ones. Whether it was old material from hand-me-downs I don't know, but I was very well dressed. To our mother Emily's dying day she always averred that fact. Underwear, frilly petticoats, ribbons, buttons and bows – that was me. Within days of moving back into *48* many of my clothes went AWOL! Our large family at *48* was share and share alike. It was a bit of a rude awakening. Even the extended family of numerous cousins profited eventually as I grew out of all that nice finery from Wales, and I wore the hand-me-downs from others. Rationing did not end in 1945.

I now shared a double bed with four sisters, three at the top end and two at the bottom end. There was a single bed in the same back bedroom which Matilda slept in. The tiny boxroom was Emmie's bedroom. She was the eldest. One of the little ones slept with Matilda in the single bed. That was one and a half persons! A young sister slept on the outside of our mother. I did not know that there had been ten girls until my sisters told me. There are no photos of Thelma. Whether none were taken or whether Mother or Father destroyed them in their grief we do not know. Mother when asked (in 1993) just said there were none. My eldest three sisters remember Thelma very well; they looked after her. She was very beautiful and looked like sister number nine.

Time went on as it always does, and like the tide it waits for no man. Each sister that wed vacated the box room for the next eldest sister at home. I was a married woman long before the sixth of Mother's ten daughters. At nineteen years of age I married my beloved Fred and I moved from *48* and never ever slept there again.

I have been told many stories about life in Stepney when I lived there as a toddler. Different sisters have come up with various accounts, yet they all tally. Mother's stories did too.

Compared to Stepney, Dagenham, Essex, was a *luxurious* step up the ladder of their existence. Eventually the extended families moved to Essex – some at The Fiddlers and some in Romford or down the line (the line being the railways). The Fiddlers was a pub about ten minutes' walk in *high* heels. We wore *high* heels not just because it was the fashion, but because we were all so short of height; we've worn *high* heels or *high wedged shoes* all our adult lives. Matilda was four foot eleven inches then and Eileen must have been about the same or near enough.

When Emmie, our eldest sister, was about five years old Mother and her brood of girls lived at 9 Elsa Street, Stepney, again with our mother's parents and their children (Mother, Father and five children). At about eighteen months of age poor Thelma died of double pneumonia. Mother was then about twenty-two years old. Emmie and Tiny and Eileen remember someone making the girls' black-and-white check dresses to wear at Thelma's funeral. "It was a tiny white coffin with little pompoms which hung all round the top. Thelma lay in Granny's front room under the window." The children sat on the low window sill in their little funeral dresses all scrubbed and shining. Mother was a great believer in respectability. Mother had very long hair parted down the middle arranged in two long plaits, which she would bunch round her ears like earphones. She always wore a cloche hat which came down over them – the prevailing style.

Emmie remembers when she was twelve years old and our family moved to Grove Road. A better part of the slums! There was a fairground and Emmie practically lived there with her new friend, a girl, whose father operated the fair – the first time Emmie had seen *inside* a caravan. She was suitably impressed. Palling up with this friend, she managed to get lots of free fairground rides. Father got some odd jobs helping with the fairground tents and huge marquee – cash in hand. These were the years of the terrible depression, no regular work for the poorer masses and not many benefits to speak of (National Assistance).

At South Grove Buildings (multi-tenanted flats) *millions of children*, many with bare feet, nearly all in ragged hand-me-downs, played with my three eldest sisters.

Thelma was a baby and Emmie, Tiny and Eileen took her to the corner shop at Elsa Street to buy her a hokey-pokey ice cream, because Thelma loved it. The ice cream was usually made and sold by Italian hokey-pokey men. Maybe their English lingo was not too good.

Born after Thelma was Mother's fifth daughter. Every Sunday Emmie and the three younger ones went to the Mission Sunday School round the corner. People used to remark, seeing them all dressed alike, how nicely our mother dressed her daughters – an honour in that *day and age and environment*. Mother had four sisters. Some of her brood were named after them. She also had three brothers. All were very young. Uncle Bill (William) eventually ended up in a wheelchair. Supposedly he'd had polio, so the story goes. George worked a short time where material was handled. He used to get remnants for dresses for Mother's little girls.

Mother was too poor to possess her own camera – there are very few photos of her brood when living in Stepney. Mother's girls went out collecting *hopefully* for pennies on Guy Fawkes Night each year

– not just because they wanted to, but because they were told to. The girls had to take the pennies home because they were so desperately poor and needed money for food. Mother gave the children a few ha'pennies and farthings for sparklers and sweets – their *reward*. When I returned to England none of my family went to church, which was a shock to me as I was brought up for five and a half years in the Welsh Calvinist chapel at The Rock. *I no longer went to church!*

Emmie always remembers one of their favourite hymns at the Mission was 'Jesus Bids Us Shine'. In her last few letters to me before she died in 1999 our eldest sister, Emmie, penned the words: 'Mother was a pretty woman and a good woman but unfortunately she lived in the valley of hard knocks.' Emmie having been born on Mother's seventeenth birthday it was as if they were sisters. She remained in close contact with Mother all her life.

Mother's brood increased regularly and they had to have some help from the relief officer. It was very hard to get it because the RO laid down strict criteria. They called on Mother, and if there was any little thing saleable she had to sell it first!

The relief officer was a lady and she knew all the answers! Her favourite suggestion was to buy cheap marrowbones. They made a really good soup. Actually Mother was renowned all her life for her soups. She had plenty of practice. "Make sure you put the old pearl barley in" were Mother's very words. The relief officer became known as Old Marrowbones!

To fuel the fire Mother sent the girls to get some coke, lugging the old pram along to convey it home!

When the workmen were tearing up the tarry blocks from the roads Mother sent the little girls with the old pram to cart some home. Then she'd send them back out again for more. Mother chopped the wood into sticks, kept some for her own fire and then the little girls had to go with bundles of sticks in the old pram and sell them from door to door!

Emmie always said if she'd had a pound for every tarry block she'd carted home with my other sisters she'd be able to fly to England and back!

The little girls looked for the wooden egg boxes (crates) and when they found them they looked to see if there were any forgotten eggs amongst the packaging of straw (there often was) and took it or them home for Father's dinner!

Mother chopped up the egg crates and off went the sisters selling firewood again.

My sisters said they couldn't believe, on looking back, just how poor our family was! They didn't realise it because everybody else was in the same boat, only there were more of Mother's young brood than them!

As babies they went to the hop fields annually, where Mother picked to earn money and got the little ones picking too. That was how the children got their winter coats – they picked hops to pay for their coats.

The sisters went to Grove Road School, London, with our cousins, who were quite numerous! Eileen got the poker scar on her face when she was a year old.

When our family lived at Cordova Road off Grove Road, Mile End, they lived above a fish-and-chip shop, which they took on. (Mother made fish and chips for us better than the shop all her life.) It was next to Mile End Station. The house had huge heavy doors and they pushed huge bolts and a heavy iron bar across both doors. Tiny started sleepwalking. Mother heard the bar rattling and woke up. They put Tiny to sleep at the bottom of their bed.

In the basement lived a little family – a mother, father and little curly-headed boy. The father was minus some fingers! The little boy caught *his fingers* in his mother's heavy cast-iron mangle rollers! He had to have some of *his* fingers off too! Ughhh! The boy liked stale bread to dip in his tea and always asked our mum for stale bread. Mother rarely had any left with her large brood!

Emmie, the eldest daughter, took three sisters and herself to school at Grove Road School. On Sundays of course she had to take them to the Mission Sunday School (it got them out of Mother's way for a while!) and as they turned the corner they sang a little ditty Emmie had made up.

> 'O Come to the Mission, will you come?
> Bring your own cup 'n' saucer and a bun.
> The preacher will be there, to say a little prayer –
> So come to the Mission, will you come?'

The *girls* have vivid memories of poor little Thelma's death and funeral. Tiny remembers it because it was when she had her first ever nosebleed sitting on the pavement outside Granny Robinson's rented *house*, where they lived with Granny and Grandad and their younger brood! The girls were wearing red velvet dresses (they got the material from Uncle) and were eating cherries, Tiny pushed a cherry pip up her nose and was dragged to the clinic to have the pip removed!

Thelma was sitting in her pushchair when a girl named Elsie took hold of Thelma's finger and bit it. The poor baby screamed, springing back in the pushchair so violently it tipped over, cracking Thelma's head on the hard pavement. Tiny was about four or five then. After that incident Thelma caught double pneumonia and died. Her little white coffin was placed under the seat of the coach driver of the hearse. The big black horses with their gorgeous deep-purple plumes sadly bore her away.

Emmie and Tiny screamed, wanting to go with their baby sister! To placate them, Mother's youngest sister, Auntie Ada, took them to a toy shop – a *sort of* toyshop – and bought them a penny celluloid doll each!

The tragedy precipitated another move for our parents: this time to the large house on the corner of Grove Road and Cordova Road. A feather-pillows factory situated at the end of the road intrigued the children. Covered in feathers, the factory girls went into a corner shop at lunchtime to buy penny slices of corned beef, a slice of bread and a *ha'p'orth* of pickle. Literally! People were so dirt poor that was how they shopped! A penn'orth of jam or a ha'pennyworth of something else or a farthing's worth of something. Later when I was teaching adults I was told this over and over again by *very* elderly students. Nobody looked down on anyone as everyone was in the same boat. They said it was the *normal thing* to do. Matilda told me the girls from the factory were smothered in feathers flying around them!

In London, as young as the girls were, Mother sent them over to Victoria Park, telling them not to come home before five in the late afternoon, so they were out all day. Mother made up a big bottle of lemonade and some bread and jam sandwiches and some home-made bread pudding, which Mother made from stale bread from the local baker. It was delicious. Off went the girls with baby Violet (me) in the old battered pram – spotless of course, the pram and the girls. They had to ask people the time because naturally they were too poor to have the luxury of a wristwatch. I was now six months old and the sister above me was toddling along at approximately two years of age. The sister above her was about four years old, with Eileen (Thelma had died years earlier) eight, Matilda ten and Emmie twelve. The older girls cared for the younger ones at all times when not attending school. They knew no different – it was the way of their world. What an awesome responsibility in their tender years, but it never fazed them!

Eileen said that any time they had a nasty fall Mother took a Steedman's packet of powder from her handbag and gave it to them. If she was not with them they had to tell her as soon as they got home. What Steedman's powder did for them is not apparent. Maybe it was for shock!

Having lost daughter number four, Thelma, Mother would have been more worried about falls.

Mother's brood of girls all had thick, luxurious, very dark-brown or black hair except the tenth daughter, who was strawberry blonde. We used to tease Mother and said she must have been the milkman's daughter (a Cockney waggish saying). Mother would roar with laughter and say, "I'm going to kick his cart!"

Our mother was a fantastic knitter. We were all taught to knit our own jumpers, skirts and cardigans. Mother used to knit us little skirts and attach them to a cotton top. We wore the jumpers over the tops and the skirts fitted little bodies better that way.

Mother rubbed margarine into the girls' best shoes, handed down from one girl to another as they were grown out of, to prevent them from cracking.

When I was several months old our mother's youngest sister was married. Matilda and our cousin Maudie were bridesmaids. Matilda was a popular choice as a bridesmaid and lost count of how many times, disproving the lyrics of the popular Cockney song 'Why Am I Always the Bridesmaid and Never the Blushing Bride?'.

Whenever Mother chopped up firewood to sell, her youngest brother, Dickie, helped the girls lugging it from door to door, selling it for a few coppers a bundle of kindling. It helped to pay for food, especially for Father's dinner!

Dickie was about the same age as Emmie, but he was actually our young uncle.

On the top floor of our tenement slum building there was another large family. The father was full of the milk of human kindness, until our parents moved away – 'going up the ladder' was Mother's familiar saying. The old man used to give our family large bowls of fish.

Our family in retrospect did move many times, in the same building or nearby, eventually progressing to better parts of London tenancies.

The girls were always working for small change, running errands for better-off people (not much better off), looking after other little children whilst their parents were down the pub, or having quiet adult time together.

Mother put milk stout (beer) in her puddings. I never saw Mother use a cookery book – never saw one in the house. She made wonderful dinners with a taste of their own.

Father blacked the girls' faces for Guy Fawkes Night to disguise them. They didn't want people to think the Humphreys girls were begging, did they? In effect they were. Most families did and we thought nothing of it. Sometimes it was hard to tell which was the Guy Fawkes from some of the ragged urchins and who was the child.

Holes were pierced in tins and string was threaded through. The sisters rattled the cans hopefully in front of people outside pubs, bus stops and cinemas, the latter being the most lucrative. "Penny for the guy, mister." It never failed. Bronze change then was large and very heavy. In next to no time the cans filled up. One of the sisters then ran home to Mother, who emptied it into her purse! Then they ran back again to once more rattle their cans. It sounds terrible now, but during the depression years it was dog eat dog to get food for the children.

When I returned to live again in England I recall doing the Guy Fawkes Night stint. It was a novelty to me. By then of course it was a *tradition* and we kept the money ourselves.

Cinemas were in their heyday. You were *somebody* if you were a cinema manager. Cinemas were the last word in *luxury* in the days of the *dirt poor* and the other levels of poverty which existed side by side. The liveried *doorman* wore white gloves, and a smart cap, heavily braided. He ushered you through the doors of his exotic premises. The chandeliered lighting and the very *scent* of the cinemas transported everyone into a lifestyle which most people knew they would never achieve. But one could *dream* and the cinemas peddled those lovely dreams, giving the poor aspirations of *going up the ladder*. No, they would not achieve the same heights as their heroes and heroines of the *silver screen*, but it kept their spirits up. The trip to the cinema gave them something to lighten their bleak lives, especially during the depression years. So popular were cinemas that some people cheated and saw the films twice around! The queues stretched and doubled all round the cinema building itself. It was nothing unusual to wait two hours to get inside. Lucrative pickings on Guy Fawkes Nights! What bloke could resist the little beggars? Who could resist showing off to his girlfriend with a rattle of coppers into the tin cans? There was friendly rivalry to see who could be the most *generous show-off* to the cheeky little blighters.

A family were known to be *on the fiddle*. He was called Teapot, for some obscure reason! Maybe he kept money in the teapot? Their eldest son had a calliper on his leg. The old man had a shed on the corner of Maplin Street (where Matilda's future in-laws lived). He had a finger in many pies, and one was teddy bears! Mother used to do some work at home stuffing the teddy bears with straw. Eileen had little fingers and was made to stuff the ears! Mother was paid for the work, but the girls weren't! Their coppers had to go to Mother. Her excuse for them working with her was that she *knew* where they were!

43

The coalman lifted sacks of coal from his coal cart and humped it away on his hefty shoulders. Our sister picked up a piece of folded paper on top of the horse's dung! She obediently took it to Mother. It was a ten shilling note (50p) – a small *fortune*, a windfall!

Granny found a penny under the bed and gave it to Eileen, who went to the shop in Maplin Street for dips (sherbets with a straw). The lady put them in a shoebox and Eileen took them to Mother, to be shared.

Mother sent the children to Granny with two shillings (10p now!) and told them to tell Granny to get a leg of lamb! The Old Market was open till nine o'clock at night.

We had an Auntie Alice and an Auntie Emmie living down the same road. There were so many uncles and cousins I have given up trying to work out who was who. To this day I do not know. My younger sister knows more of them than me. She often sees our late aunt's family at Romford Market. They still run fruit and vegetable stalls there, passed down from generation to generation like the Fowlers in the television programme *EastEnders*.

On special days like bank holidays our mother gave my older sisters (still very young) a few coppers so they could ride on trams all day – a day out!

Their abode was very damp and sister Queenie got rheumatic fever. It left her with a weakened heart (she died in 1991 at her home in Australia; she was only sixty). I never knew about the rheumatic fever until recent years. Mother was told she *would grow out of it*. It was never alluded to when I lived at *48*.

She got breast cancer when living in Australia. She'd had an operation and been told she had another five years to live. Within weeks she was dead from a heart attack. We all feel very sad about that. We loved her.

In the early days of hop-picking when still living in Limehouse, Stepney and Mile End, Mother and her brood travelled to the hop fields of Kent and Sussex by steam train. It was their annual *holiday*. Mother was a good picker; so were her brood. She made them all pick! As a *reward* she was allocated two huts each year! Big deal! They would camp in those corrugated huts for as many weeks as it took to pick the fat hops, depending on the weather. If it was sunny the hops were plump and easier to pluck from the hop bines. We picked in inclement weather, but if it was torrential the hops *sulked*. It was difficult to pluck them then. Drizzle or showers was OK. Either way the fields ran with muddy water and thick mud. The hop bines were growing from long banked-up ridges of earth. Our hop bin, made of sacking and wooden ends of crossed spars, was situated inside two rows of bines. We moved along, pulling down and tugging the bines, and slung them over the bins so we could pluck the hops. Other pickers were in the next rows all over the hop fields. If a family of *good pickers* finished their row quickly they were entitled to go into the next row and work their way up to those going down from the front. Very friendly rivalry ensued for the plumpest hops. The steam-train *hop-pickers* went from London Bridge. Quite a sight! All those hundreds of people with their old tea chests filled with bedding, clothes, pots and pans and everything necessary for the weeks at the hop fields!

Father made a *carriage* from an old pram chassis. He fixed a huge empty tea chest on it. In those days empty tea chests were easy to come by. Emmie and Matilda and little Eileen had to shove that contraption loaded up "with everything portable," they said . . . all the way to London Bridge. The place was swarming with people and their tea chests and bags and bundles. With hordes of the poorest of the poor East Enders mixed up with the not so poor! It meant good clean fresh country air for the urchins' poor starved lungs – a holiday from the slums, green fields to play in, rabbits to poach and cooking apples to be scrumped by the sackful. 'Hopping apples' were the largest cooking apples I have ever seen. In a sack to bring back home after hopping ended for the year they had an aroma never forgotten. They were supposed to be *windfalls*, but we took *that* with a pinch of salt!

The camaraderie of hop-picking was absolutely wonderful. I cannot think of anyone who has been hopping who has not enjoyed the whole experience of living in huts and using outside *makeshift* loos.

In later years our family travelled from *48* to the hop fields by open lorries. They did have tarpaulins if it rained; otherwise we all stood up holding on to the lorry all the way to the hop fields and our two hopping huts. It was the greatest of fun times. No motorways – we went through towns and villages waving at everyone. We had another family or two sharing our lorry. The men and boys whistled shrilly at every pretty female they saw. I can still hear them in my memories, but could not hear the whistles after I lost my hearing in December 1946. Bowling along, we sang with gusto all the old-time music-hall songs and the hopping song 'Old Mother Riley Who Had a Fat Cow'. I can still *hear* that singing.

When our family still lived in the East End of London Matilda used to look after four McCarthy children each week for a few coppers. Matilda was only about nine years old. She also got shopping for their mother.

When Mr and Mrs McCarthy went to the cinema – or local fleapit, as it was jokingly termed – they paid Matilda thruppence in old money. Mother always took those coppers to pay for a hot meal for Father – Mother was scared not to have money for his hot dinner.

In those far-off days men were a law unto themselves because legally wives were mere chattels. The hot dinner for a man whether or not he was working was compulsory. Women were fearful if their husbands did not have a hot meal. Mother was no exception – she thought the same way.

One day Mother sent six-year-old Eileen to see if Matilda had a few coppers. The McCarthys hadn't yet left home to go to the cinema. Mrs McCarthy was enraged. Up the stairs she flew to our tenement hovel of a flat and had an almighty row with Mother. "I don't give Tiny a few coppers just to feed your old man his dinner!"

Matilda was never again asked to look after the McCarthy children. Each week it had been eight-year-old Tiny's coppers which had paid for Father's hot dinner one day a week, whilst the girls got bread and jam for a ha'porth a dollop from a shop nearby, or bones soup.

Amongst the poor downtrodden East Enders there were always moneylenders. It was either them or the pawnshop with its three hanging brass balls. Moneylenders charged extortionate rates of interest over a length of time. There was one such called Sunshine or Blindshine. The women used the money to feed, clothe and shoe their large broods, to pay the rent and to get food for their husbands' daily hot dinner.

Sometimes when Mother heard Blindshine's stick tap-tapping up the stairs she got the wind up (frightened) and sent one of the girls to the door to say, "Mum's not in today."

Whenever a dollop bought or made something the girls did not like she would say, "Old Blindshine would be glad to see it."

Every day Mother scrubbed everything – herself, her brood and the floors – and wiped the walls down. It was the best way of keeping disease at bay, living in such a close-proximity habitat. Some days she would start doing the washing in the old round tin bath (no bathrooms in the tenements) at 7 a.m. and finish at 9 p.m., stopping to feed and change babies and to cook Father's hot dinner. With her trusted scrubbing board made of strong wood and tough rippled glass, and with her arms and elbows deep in soapy suds from shavings of her precious bar of Sunlight soap, she'd be singing merrily with hopefully a pan of bones and vegetable soup bubbling merrily on a gas ring.

The girls played with two children, Colleen and Colin, and their relative who used their home as an illegal betting shop. Now and again the police raided, chasing him. The police would force themselves into all the homes in the tenement buildings, trying to catch him with alleged betting slips.

The term 'the good old days' had a downside to it in almost every way for the very poor citizens.

When it was time for Father's hot dinner, Mother sent the girls to find him. He was often at the billiards hall.

Mother loved watching wrestling matches (she watched them on television in the years yet to come), and when there was one near them she ordered the girls to take a chair up to the roof, where she would sit watching the match peacefully and enthusiastically with baby Violet (me) on her lap. I must admit wrestling is not my cup of tea. As the saying goes, 'Each to their own!'

Before we and the numerous aunts, uncles, cousins and friends left the tenements for better parts of London or to settle in Essex – going up the ladder – Mother's youngest brother, Richard, known as Dickie, joined the Territorials. It was because he wanted some good clothes to wear – the uniform. One day when he turned up at Granny's home, starving hungry as usual, all she could give him to eat was crumpets. She was now too poor to spare any food for her adult children!

Sometimes Mother accompanied her girls on their way to school and she'd call in a wool shop to buy some oddments of coloured wool cheaply (pure wool). I have an old photo of little Doreen wearing a Fair Isle jumper which I had knitted for her when I was about eleven. Matilda, in adult life, knitted the most beautiful Fair Isle pullovers in intricate patterns for her husband, Harry. All of Emily's daughters became splendid knitters using fancy patterns (not Fair Isle) and plain ones – jumpers, cardigans, skirts, jackets and two-piece costumes on a circular needle; socks on four needles. Our mother's teaching stood us in good stead all our lives.

When Maudie, our mother's sister, and a brother went to Canada hoping for a better life of opportunities, Mother, Father and their brood were designated to sail with them. At the last minute Mother refused to go on the boat and returned to the tenement! Fate could have meant different lives for us girls and I would not have become deaf! the Lord God moves in mysterious ways. Eventually our auntie and uncle came back.

CHAPTER SEVEN

For poor Mother the babies kept coming almost as regular as clockwork, with roughly two years between each one. It was a bit closer than two years with Emmie, Matilda, Eileen and Thelma.

Someone up above smiled down on Mother and her brood and they were moved to the Heathway, Dagenham, Essex. *Gradually climbing the ladder of poverty!* It was the girls' wages and Mother's later on which propelled the family further *up the ladder*. The Second World War meant full employment again in the armaments and clothing sections of the joint war effort in Great Britain.

Again fortune smiled down on her and they moved into a house in Dagenham, Essex, ever after called *48*. Prior to that move Queenie had gone to a *special* school at the top of the Heathway and the girls went to Eastbrook School. It was about a mile there and back to walk each weekday.

They were still relatively poor, but not destitute! War had not yet been officially declared, but it was *in the offing*. A bicycle was still a luxury and so were roller skates, which clipped on to any-sized shoes. Father managed to have an old '*boneshaker*' bicycle to whizz around on – a sit-up-and-beg bicycle. The streets were practically devoid of anything with a combustion engine. The Cockney's pushcart with its *flat bed* was still the main form of transporting one's goods or wares. They were handy items when pushed by a hefty bloke, or pulled along.

At *48* there was a gaslight outside the front bedroom window. They never had to switch the light on in that room. The light shone through the drawn unlined curtains. In those days the poor if they had curtains did not line them.

Pettits Place, where they lived at the Heathway, was not home for long. One year they went hopping by lorry and and when they returned at the end of the *hopping season* our family went straight into the new house. It had three bedrooms and a bathroom – luxury

– a small kitchen, just big enough for Mother (we had to squeeze past her), a back living room and a front best living room, a small garden at the front and a large, long back garden. Father got his own chicken coops at long last! The family diet was now supplemented with protein-rich chicken on tap. It was the older girls who cleaned out the coops and fed the chickens, of course.

Father bought newborn chicks and reared them at first in an old tea chest. Tea chests were easy to obtain. They held loose tea until it went to the factories to be sorted and packaged for the shops. Father rigged an open electric light bulb over the top of the tea chest and the warmth of the bulb had the chicks huddling beneath it. When they were old enough they went into the coop in the back garden, eventually for our Sunday dinner and their carcass for a nourishing soup.

Our parents lived in that house until they died. Father died in a nursing home in Ilford after several months living there. Mother died suddenly at sister number six's flat in Hanworth, although she had not wanted to visit there. The sister heard nothing, but found her dead in the bathroom when she arose the next morning to go to work. It was a very sudden death. I managed to obtain a post-mortem from the authorities, and my own GP explained it to me.

At *48* it was fun to watch the lamplighter cycle up to the lamp posts in the street and light them at dusk. The lamp post had a metal *arm* for the man to rest his little ladder against for safety. Up he'd climb, then he'd set off again with his ladder tucked under his arm, nonchalantly whistling up one street and down another. I remember he had a very loud whistle.

We could hear Mother when we were playing in the road. She would start calling our names until she came to the correct one(!), yelling, "Queenie, Eileen . . ."

If her daughters turned a deaf ear someone was sure to yell out exultantly, " Yer muvver's callin' yer!"

Standing at the front door, which was usually open as was the norm in those days, Mother would hear the milkman and his float in the next street and send one of us to pick up a pint so she could have her cup of tea. By the time the milkman had finished chatting to his customers and got round to our door the pot of tea would be stone cold!

The streets were full of children – in Wales as in England. If your own children were not in sight and the children were too noisy the mums called out, "'Ere, y'little sods, go 'n' play down yer own end." The children obeyed until someone else sent them back again. Backwards and forwards they went like a ping-pong ball until they got fed up and went to torment another street with their noisy games.

At Gerald Road, where *48* was and still is, the children got their *revenge* with *knock-down Ginger*. After dark they tied strings to door knockers, hid themselves and pulled the strings. 'Knock! Knock! Knock! Knock!' Irate householders opening their front doors several times would be jeered cheerfully and non-maliciously with cries of "*Knock-down Ginger!*" I never did fathom out how they got the name. The householder, usually the man of the house, might laugh it off and be bothered no more that night, or he might yell blue murder and be pestered for hours. Most were good-humoured.

In my memory banks I still *hear* the sound of the door knockers being thumped in *knock-down-Ginger* games. There was always at least one young fella brave enough to actually tiptoe up a garden path and then give a *thundering double knock* and flee for his life before the door was flung open and the passage light streamed from it. By then we'd scarpered – if we were fast enough! Or it was a simple matter to loop a long string through the handle of the door knocker; then we'd *play out* the string to its full length and *lift and drop* the knocker. But that was too easy! The householders usually knew the *sound* of a *knock-down-Ginger* letter-box *drop*. Great sport – those days of our innocent youth!

There was a row of *everyday shops* along the main road at the top of Winifred Road: butcher, baker, sweet shop and others. We used to say *run up the top and get this or that*. Opposite the shops was the bus stop and the road to our primary school, Grafton Road School. We always went on our own. It was *safer* in those days – less traffic too.

After the war, as time went by and the girls were bringing home good wages, the house, *48*, was purchased by our parents.

Our family have come a long way from the slums of Limehouse, Stepney, Mile End and the Heathway. My sisters have worked all their lives. Emmie was a GI war bride and lived in the USA (she died in 1999) and Tiny (Matilda), who lives in Coventry, and Eileen, in Essex, have memories going back the furthest to our life of poverty in the tenement buildings of Stepney, in the East End of London. I'm using a little of their memories in the first few chapters to show what life was really like before the war. It's been an eye-opener for me. I added their accounts for sociological and historical accuracy.

As I sit here today I know we have lost seven of Mother's lovely girls whom I was proud to call my sisters – especially Emmie, Matilda, Eileen and Queenie, the four eldest. They aided me wonderfully when the unexpected time of silence began for me.

It was just a shock for myself and everyone and we all had to acclimatise ourselves to the situation. I cannot praise my family enough for doing their utmost to help me carry on enjoying life. I had only returned to the fold the year before after being away from age four to nine and a half with no contact visually or by phone in all that time.

One certainly learns to adapt out of necessity. Between us my sisters and I have had twenty-five children, mostly boys!

Myself, here in 2018, I have two sons, four grandsons and one granddaughter, four great-grandsons and three great-granddaughters with another great-granddaughter due shortly.

They all enjoy normal hearing despite Fred and me being deaf.

Doreen, Mother's ninth daughter, had the largest family of us girls – four sons and three daughters, with Patricia, the last of the seven children, dying upon birth.

Nobody emulated Mother's large brood.

Undoubtedly the world looks different from our memories. I am reminded of some of Dylan Thomas's poems: '*as I was young and easy . . .*' It's good to look back, and God in His infinite wisdom colours some of our memories with a rosy glow! We tend to recall the good and push the bad bits away. There's nothing wrong in that: it's all part and parcel of our lives.

In the far-off poverty days of Stepney (and round about then) it is sad to think that there was no National Health Service. It never came into being until 1948. The National Health Service has served me very well from a personal point of fact. I am tremendously grateful for the NHS. Apart from my seven miscarriages, I have at a quick count been an inpatient in my lifetime at the following hospitals in England: Romford Isolation Hospital; the London Hospital, Whitechapel; the Ear, Nose and Throat Hospital; the Royal Homeopathic Hospital; Plaistow Hospital; and the Queen Elizabeth. Additionally I was an outpatient at other hospitals – many times at the East Ham Memorial Hospital. I was born in the Bancroft Road hospital, Mile End. That could be the hospital where I went at one year old with pneumonia, but I forgot to ask my mother and older sisters before they all died.

Those were the glorious days of the hospital matron! They ran tight ships, but they were magnificent at running their hospitals. We should bring them back! We felt incredibly safe inside the long wards. The Sisters and nurses under the matron's rule were exemplary. We had respect and trust in the Sisters. If we were worried about anything they were never too busy to find a minute to discuss it. I can still see the brass bell being swung in the hands of one of the junior nurses, imploring us to chuck our visitors out or *she* would get it in the neck from the Staff Nurse – the one with the elastic black belt round her trim waist held together by her *qualified-nurse* clasp. They were absolutely great nurses . . . and the ward cleaners were marvellous too. The lavatories were spotless. The plastic aprons today may be more hygienic, but when a nurse cuddled a frightened patient it was more *cosy* to smell their starched aprons than the smell of cold plastic. They looked nicer and smarter too. My favourite nurse's uniform has to be that of the London Hospital, Whitechapel – including their headdresses and their long and colourful dresses. I used to cheer up just to see them! They gave many a fillip to a patient feeling down in the doldrums or scared. I liked the traditional uniforms with their pretty lace *loose* white cuffs on short sleeves and their pert little old-fashioned caps. I always tell people about the Whitechapel hospital nurses' uniform. Being long it made for modesty when they had to bend and lift people. I don't know if they still have the same long uniforms now as they did before I moved to Norfolk. I sincerely hope they are still wearing their traditional garments. Bless them.

CHAPTER EIGHT

My England! Home of my ancestors as far back as I know on Father's side, who seem to have been mostly Londoners. On Mother's side it has recently been discovered that we also go back on a French side as far back as 1594! Her family married into French families or family along the way after many escaped to live in England.

Life is queer with its twists and turns, as each one of us sometimes learns.

What changes we have seen since the Second World War. The Russian astronaut, Yuri Gagarin, was the first man to travel in space. The Americans were first to actually land on the moon and make their historic walk.

Biros, automatic washing machines, drying machines, fridges available to the masses, videos, camcorders, mobile phones, Tablets, computers in most homes, widescreen colour televisions, better medicines and medical operations, lung and heart transplants, blood banks, marrow banks, strong painkillers, paramedics, flying medics, defibrillators . . . The list is almost endless, not forgetting the wonder of the Internet, drones, gadgets which have revolutionised a woman's housework and relieved the old-time drudgery of it, CDs, DVDs, and wet rooms instead of bathrooms.

We girls never had these in our early lives, most of which are taken for granted today.

So many things undreamed of when I returned to England in 1945 gradually came to pass and are now part and parcel of our lives wherever we live. The war years were bleak – very bleak – but life goes on and *Homo sapiens* learns to adapt and tolerate. One of the biggest changes of course has been the ease of divorce. It's good in some ways that incompatible people are no longer *tied for life*, but bad for children, who have their whole childhoods disrupted by anger and in many cases deep bitterness. Everyone loses out. Happily it is no longer a stigma to divorce. Women have more equality in life. Yes, it is supposed to be *all* equality, but in practice that is not always true.

I am delighted women are officially no longer mere *chattels* – something to celebrate.

On the down side we now have different deadly incurable diseases in our country. The pill has brought sexual freedom, but made it harder for girls to say *no* and mean it. How this problem will be eradicated I know not. Many may not see it as a *problem*, but it is in some ways and it's made worse with global freedom of travel. I do not want to give an opinion on this – I am not qualified to do so. The greatest change has been for women's freedom and the rise of the six-figure-sum-per-annum working career woman.

In 1945 I met my youngest sister for the first time (born in 1942) and I got to know baby Doreen (born in March 1940). She was now a five-year-old child and I was nine and a half. Our English family of girls had a *playmate* whom they adored as the *baby*: Peggy the Pekinese mongrel, for want of a better description. We still speak affectionately of the dog, and another acquired years later. One day poor Peggy slipped out through the front gate. She was in *heat* and the dogs got her and tore her to pieces.

The next dog was the last until Mother was elderly. That was Tangy. She was a peke, but not so much loved. Mother had an awful rat-looking skinny chihuahua who died a few years before Mother. She was always yapping and a nuisance as far as we were concerned, but Mother loved her Peggy, the chihuahua. Two sisters came over from America and brought Mother down to see me in Norfolk. Peggy came too.

At *48* apart from the chickens we kept rabbits – for eating. You couldn't afford to be too sentimental in a large family when it came to food! Father also grew potatoes, lettuces, radishes, spring onions, and other bits in the back garden. We were self-sufficient with tomatoes. When green they were wrapped in newspaper, placed in an airing cupboard and hey presto! fresh tomatoes. Mother would say, "Pop upstairs and get me a few tomatoes."

The older schoolgirls went to school at Triptons after Grafton Road School. I was looking forward to going there. It was on the corner of Tenterden Road and the main road. At the other end were the tank traps – edifices of concrete to stop enemy tanks if they invaded us. The plan was for the civic-centre staff to run the area from the school if the centre was bombed. It never happened.

There was a pub called the Merry Fiddlers. You'd say to the

bus conductor, "*Fiddlers, please.*" You gave him the fare and he punched you a coloured thin *cardboard* bus ticket.

There were shops *up the Fiddlers*, including a smashing takeaway fish-and-chip shop, which is still there!

Everybody went to the cinema. You waited in the queue for the cinema. After you came out you joined another long queue for your fresh fish and chips or a ha'p'orth of *crackling* – the bits of batter left after fish was cooked. Delicious!

Bus stops at the Fiddlers took you all over the place. Buses went to Romford in Essex or to London . . . everywhere. You see, *48* was in a neat position for a family. And the railways were on the bus routes too. Public transport was much cheaper and reasonable in those times.

The back garden at *48* was for the washing, the poultry rearing, the rabbits for stew, and the vegetables. We girls played in the streets. For some reason our parents did not like us going into the garden. Of course we went out there to use the huge iron mangle, whose thick heavy rollers of wood made the wet sheets look as if they had been ironed and folded. The garden was always neat and tidy because we were not encouraged to go out there, except for special reasons. The streets were car-less and our playgrounds. The air-raid shelter had yet to be removed when I got back. It smelt dank and was dark and gloomy and ankle-deep in water.

Auntie and her husband were bombed out during the war, and with Granny and Grandad they moved in with us. There were now fourteen people sleeping in Mother's little air-raid shelter! Number *48* had only three bedrooms for fourteen people (I was in Wales).

The silver-coloured tin was kept inside by the air-raid *door*, only it was a blanket not a door (better if there was a bomb blast). The family particulars were kept in that box – that was just our parents and us. If there had been a direct hit nobody would have known about the extra adults.

Emmie, Tiny and Eileen were working and I joined the three little ones at Grafton Junior School.

Some years later Father was out of work for many years, smothered in gauze and creams and bandages. He had learnt plastering and caught dermatitis on his face, body, legs, arms . . . everywhere. Horrible! Maybe that's the reason Mother never fell for any more babies!

Mother went out to work at various jobs, ending up at Ever Ready batteries until she was sixty. Father was now able to see to the three youngest ones and get them off to school each day, on their own. He did not do the housework or cooking, apart from frying an egg or two for his lunch – he was quite *talented* at *that* job. He still did the decorating with Mother's help. Every year in the run-up to Christmas the house was decorated! It was a *throwback habit* from their years in the overcrowded tenements of Stepney, where there was always a fear of diseases. First the wallpaper was stripped with all the girls helping. We always got the *rotten jobs*, or our mother did. Then all the paintwork was washed down with sugar soap, including the nice wooden mantelpiece. There was a discussion on the merits of different-coloured paints. One year they were very enamoured of a light shade of mushroom. The mantelpiece thus changed colour like a chameleon each year. After the wallpaper, it was up with the Christmas decorations. He never threw any away – some of them must be *collectors'* items now.

Father was too lazy to empty the ash pan of the all-night-burning fire. Mother did it – she would not let us – but he always opened the living-room and back door for her to take the hot ash to the metal dustbin. At least it killed any germs in the dustbin.

We had to go and collect the eggs from the coops. As soon as Mother heard them being laid she told me to go and get one for my breakfast! It felt warm and rubbery when I took it from the poor chicken, but it hardened quickly. After that I never wondered how *hard eggs* got out of a poor old hen!

Before she was put into war work our sister Emmie was a sewing apprentice at Nicholsons at the corner of Paternoster Row, in London, right by St Paul's Cathedral (torn down after the war). The company made posh clothes for posh people all over the empire – which we then had. The dress forms were kept padded with the name of the posh person. Emmie did all the finishing by hand sewing, and the repeat orders. She worked on the fourth floor, which was used as the workshop. The salesrooms were downstairs. Emmie hand sewed eight stitches to the inch.

Training Emmie were four single ladies, all in their forties or early fifties (there were many like them after the First World War), and they adored Emmie, taking her under their wings, teaching her how to speak *properly* and dress with taste and neatness. Even when Emmie went to live in North America with her American husband the ladies wrote to her until their deaths. They knitted umpteen pairs of socks for Emmie's children and posted them to the USA. Emmie said Nicholsons sold almost everything and occupied an entire corner by St Paul's Cathedral. At first Emmie earned about twelve shillings and sixpence; in new money that translates as 62½p a week! After about one year Father blew up and insisted Emmie ask for a rise in money or he would make her quit! When she was fifteen they raised her wage to sixteen shillings a week, which translates as 80p!

Matilda and Eileen and Tiny were always close to each other. They did most things together. Matilda had her fourteenth birthday down at hopping one September and she was then a *woman* like Emmie! By rights she should have returned to school until the end of the Christmas term. Mother decided (or rather Father did) otherwise and took her to get a job. Matilda wanted to do dressmaking with Emmie. Mother said, "No! You'll have to earn more money than that." Apprenticeships were traditionally for low money. (Father stopped me from doing an apprenticeship in *haute couture* when I left school at seventeen and a half.) The outcome was Matilda went to London to work by lorry! She and some other girls went to and fro by lorry. They paid no fares. Mother wanted Tiny to have no fares as the bulk of Emmie's wage went on fares. Mother kept most of Matilda's wage, letting Matilda keep two shillings a week (10p) and sixpence (2½p) for her insurance stamp. Matilda was packing dog biscuits for Spratt's of Bow Road. (What a coincidence! I worked at Spratt's, learning to be a Powers-Samas punch operator. I did not complete my training as I collapsed on a bus in 1954 and was diagnosed with multiple sclerosis at the Whitechapel hospital.)

When war broke out in 1939 the Spratt's factory was converted to packing *hard-tack* biscuits for servicemen in the armed forces. (Thousands of dogs were destroyed at the outbreak of the Second World War.) Matilda and her friends put silly love notes inside the packets of biscuits for a giggle, including their addresses, but nobody got a letter back from a serviceman. Matilda got herself a better job at De La Rue (foreign currency). She liked the job, but the air raids got worse and worse and it became too scary. When the factory got bombed she left quickly! Then she worked in a *war factory*. At seventeen years of age she tried to *join up* in the armed forces (at four feet eleven inches tall!). The war factory refused to release her to the services. They had that legal right in wartime. Matilda then earned the good sum of two pounds nineteen shillings and sixpence a week (£2.97½).

As usual our mother took all of it, giving Matilda back five shillings (25p). Each week out of her five shillings Matilda bought our mother a bar of chocolate and Father five Weights (cigarettes). Then Matilda got a rise and she added a bottle of Guinness's beer, then Mother's favourite tipple, and increased Father's cigarettes. Mother and Father always threatened the older girls if they were *walking out* (with a boyfriend): "If you bring *trouble home* [get pregnant] we'll break your necks!" It was a hypocritical stance: Father had done that to our mother.

Matilda and her friend went to the Home Guard's Dance at the civic centre by the Fiddlers, but Father and Mother and their *crowd* wanted to go to the pub, so Matilda had to be home by 8.30 to look after the little ones. The dance commenced at eight! Once she was ten minutes late and Father prevented her from going out another night.

Harry Edwards and Matilda had been to school together at age eleven. When Matilda was fifteen they started courting. Harry's dad had known us *for ever*. Emmie was the apple of our parents' eyes and they let her off a bit from the leash as she grew older, but made Matilda stay in! Often Harry was met at the door by Father. "She ain't goin' out ternight, son. Me and Muvver is goin' out." Harry had to stay and help babysit.

When Emmie reached *mobile age* she was called up. Her *papers* arrived in the day's post. The papers said it would have to be war work in factories or the land army or nursing. She was seventeen.

Father decided she was not going in any of those. She said, "How about the services, Dad?" He refused to let her go. They wanted her wages at home! Emmie then went into a factory at Plessey's making fuel pumps for aeroplanes seventy feet underground. There was a railroad (railway) taken over for that express purpose. Emmie worked at Plessey's for three years. I also worked briefly at Plessey's in the fifties in their *in-house* library of tech magazines. Emmie became engaged to Jackie, but after two years they broke up. He had been her *blind date*. Emmie used the Americanism 'set-up man'.

The friendly invasion of Americans had arrived in our island and the females went gaga over them, thinking they were *all* from Hollywood!

Emmie and Tiny were enthusiastic dancers, as were most young women in wartime – it was a break from the *grey monotony* of life even if they did have to dance female to female (most of the time) until the Americans hit these shores with their jitterbugging and *smooching, dancing cheek to cheek*.

Eileen was just as enthusiastic about dancing, but still a bit young in Father's eyes; she did her best to get out with them and not look after the little ones!

At the dances Emmie met an American pilot from Oregon and they dated for about ten months; he was 'a really sweet kind person'. One evening he suggested taking our parents out for supper (high tea). They had a lovely evening until ten o'clock. Emmie accompanied him on the bus to Romford Station. Waiting for the train a dense pea-souper fog drifted in (they were horrible fogs until the Clean Air Acts in the fifties–sixties). Fogs like that choked us awfully. We hated and feared them each winter. C.L., as the pilot was called, thought Emmie should take a taxi home. She shared it with two other girls going in the same direction. The driver somehow got turned around and headed back the way he'd come! He dropped them off at Beacontree Heath, afraid he'd lose his own way home! Emmie followed the kerb all the way home in the blackout and pea-souper fog. She put her key in the lock, but Father had bolted her out for not being home by eleven. She was twenty years old! Father's words and nasty insinuations (he clearly thought all men were like himself!) cut Emmie like a knife. Out of all the *girls,* Emmie had the closest relationship with our parents, who idolised her! Emmie spent the night with Mrs Cassiday, next door, who couldn't stand Father and would tell him so to his face.

Emmie went to stay with a friend whose husband was in war services (she lived in Romford) and she lived there for ten months. Then C.L. went back to the USA for *some R & R.* They corresponded, but he became ill and never returned to England. Emmie continued corresponding; then she met Harold, another American in the USAAF, at the Romford Palais dancing venue. They dated three months and Harold asked Emmie to go back to live at *48*; he didn't like her living with Pat, who was cheating on her husband. Harold was off to France. Emmie wrote and told C.L. Emmie and Harold corresponded for six months and he said he'd told his family he was going to propose. His sister obeyed his instructions and with his money she got a set of rings. He flew back to England from France with the rings and a bottle of champagne and they became engaged.

A December wedding was planned and a cake and everything was ready, but Harold was shipped to Germany! He didn't get back until March 1945. The December after the wedding the Americans were returned to their own country. The war was over.

I was home from evacuation too late for Emmie's wedding, but not too late for Tiny's. In August it was the celebrations for victory over Japan known as VJ day. The bonfire at the fork between Gerald and Lamberhurst Roads was the biggest I'd ever seen – the bonfire to end all bonfires and commemorate eradication of evil and war!

After the war ended there was still *conscription* and Matilda's

Harry wanted to get engaged before he entered the army. Harry heard he was being sent abroad and asked Matilda to marry him before his embarkation. They were both nineteen years old – still under the age of twenty-one. Matilda duly asked Father's official permission, without which she could not marry. Under age! Father said, "Why? Have you *got* to get married?" (Was she pregnant?) Father was visibly disappointed when Tiny said *no* – he could not give her a *ripe bollocking*. The special licence was for 4 August 1945 at St Mary's Church, a short walk away. A special licence meant Father signing again. All hell broke loose. "I've signed one paper and I ain't signing another," roared Father.

It was now up to Mother to *make* Father sign the paper. Harry was one of us – he'd known us before we were born, more or less. His mum and dad, Harry and Nellie, went to the pub and the hop fields and everything else with our extended family.

Down to his garden shed stormed Father, leaving Tiny and her girlfriend sitting crying! Mother, undaunted, marched down to the shed with pen and paper and made Father sign!

Mrs Cassiday, next door, made the wedding cake; our parents paid nothing. Mr and Mrs Edwards, Harry's parents, paid for practically everything. Like all wartime brides, Tiny borrowed her wedding clothes. The shoes were a size five; Tiny normally wore a four, but she stuffed them with newspaper! Queenie, Eileen and Annie Edwards wore borrowed bridesmaids' clothes and accessories. They came from Tiny's friend, who had borrowed them from somebody else! When Tiny's friend was married two weeks later Tiny was *her* bridesmaid in one of *those* dresses. Even Matilda's wedding bouquet was utilised by her friend. War and the ensuing shortages afterwards entailed borrowing finery for weddings for most people. Matilda and Harry's honeymoon was short – three days. Then he embarked for Egypt on His Gracious Majesty's service in the army.

At *48* Matilda slept downstairs in an ancient bed-chair, origins and age unknown! Matilda and Queenie had a silly *falling-out* over the cost of a pair of dance tickets. Father lost his *rag* and bade Matilda in no uncertain tones to be gone, lock, stock and barrel, before he got home that night. Matilda was now Harry's chattel and Father could not push her around. Mother could not take most of her wages any more. Yes, Matilda was *only nineteen*, but the law is the law and she was now a married woman. Matilda was *over the moon*. She couldn't get out fast enough – cycling to her in-laws' house at Warley Avenue, telling them about Father and what he had said. (We had no telephones – most people didn't.)

I helped Matilda and Harry's Uncle George with a flat-topped costermonger's borrowed handcart to take Matilda's pathetically small belongings and her wedding presents, and her *bottom drawer*, to Warley Avenue, where her in-laws lived.

In a fiendishly hypocritical display of *helpfulness*, Father carried out the huge tea chest filled with Matilda's precious collection of china and other things. He turned the tea chest upside down and nearly killed himself laughing as everything tumbled on to the pavement and crockery was smashed to smithereens. It was deliberate – getting the *last word*, so to speak.

Matilda said, "He didn't know what a *good turn* he'd done me by chucking me out."

The Edwards family took no money from Matilda and she saved Harry's army wives' pay of two pounds nineteen shillings and sixpence until she'd enough for a deposit on some smart *utility* furniture. Under wartime austerity conditions the making of furniture was plain but serviceable. Auntie and Uncle helped her in her choice and they kept it for her until Harry came home from Egypt. Each week Matilda went to Barking and faithfully paid the instalments on her furniture: a bedroom suite, a dining-room suite and two large very plain armchairs.

In 1946 I went with our parents to see our eldest and much loved sister, Emmie, sail from Southampton to the USA – one of thousands of GI brides to be reunited with their now demobbed wartime husbands. Emmie was not *too happy* about leaving for an unknown country and a *barely known foreign husband*. Many tears were shed as she boarded the *bride* ship. She had no babies, but there were many babies sailing with their parents. Some of the reunions in America were not very successful, but others were. There were 400 brides with Emmie. Some starry-eyed GI brides found a husband out of uniform didn't look so attractive, and many were *of certainty* not from Hollywood and the film-star world! Most women had never been further than the nearest seaside back home!

The SS *Argentina* sailed into New York and alongside the Statue of Liberty. Descending the gangplank, nervous and apprehensive, Emmie saw Harold waving excitedly to his beautiful raven-haired wife. They fell into each other's arms. Emmie said Harold looked *very different* out of uniform. His whole family was with him – his mother and two sisters, Christina and Gracie, and their husbands had travelled the long distance to New York by car from Indiana.

Emmie wrote home to England and sent parcels of food, clothing and luxuries to all of us. Every week Emmie's letters and parcels were received with joy. She kept this up faithfully until our parents' deaths. And she paid for them to stay with her.

Eventually Harold built a hairdressing salon on to their farmhouse ranch. They called it Nan's Vanity Box. Nan was Harold's nickname for Emmie. Emmie qualified under strict American rules and regulations.

Customers always asked Emmie, "Where did you learn to speak good English?" So Emmie asked the customers what language they spoke and they replied *American*. Emmie cringed when she heard English badly spoken. The ladies at Nicholsons had taught Emmie such good English she'd left her Cockney language behind. If someone said *I seen* instead of *I saw* or used a preposition at the end of a sentence it made Emmie feel like shrieking!

I speak very good English. We did have speech lessons at both of my schools for the deaf. Sometimes when my husband, Fred, and I were in Trafalgar Square foreigners made a beeline to ask *me* where something was, or to ask for directions to somewhere. Fred could handle that part, for my sense of *direction* has always been poor!

My Fred was very Cockney in his speech, or at least in the sound of it, whereas I, having been retaught speech after becoming deaf, spoke good Queen's English. I intervened in my best *posh voice* and they would say, "My dear, where are you from? Where did you learn to speak such good English?" (A compliment to my schoolteachers!)

Father died in 1991, my Fred died in 1991, Queenie died in 1991 and so did some others of our relatives. None were related deaths. It was just a year of deaths (five). Our mother died in 1994; our sister Emmie died in 1999; her husband, Harold, followed her to his death one day short of a month after her. Mother had been married since 1923 and Emmie had been married since 1945 – long marriages.

Our parents are buried at Eastbrook Cemetery, in a double grave. Poor Mother – even in death she couldn't get away from Father!

I saw Mother before her sudden death, three weeks previously. My eldest son and his wife drove from North-East England, a round trip of approximately 600 miles, picked me up and took me to 48 to see Mother the same day! Mother lived about ninety miles from my home in Norfolk. Mother was fine, but she wanted home-made bread and home-made rice pudding. I took them a large home-made cake. My son's wife took two of her large home-made quiches. Just after that, at a sister's flat in Middlesex, poor Mother passed away – not in her own home, as she wanted. She died on the Monday just after her eighty-seventh birthday on 16 February, which was also the date of sister Emmie's seventieth birthday.

On Mother's last birthday I was telling her how I had just had my will updated since my husband's death and Mother said, "What for?" She insisted the law would give her daughters (!) the house between all of them and she was not leaving a will.

It didn't work out the way Mother said!

CHAPTER NINE

With Father out of work after contracting the disease dermatitis from the plaster, he got compensation, but I don't know how much. They purchased a bedroom suite and a few other things with it. He was home all day and able to get the three young ones ready for school. They went together on their own without him. Because of being at home, he was different with the three youngest and they have *nicer memories* of Father than we have. They were too young to know any different.

At term time I was at boarding school. I had been fortunate to pass the entrance examination to the Mary Hare Grammar School at the age of thirteen. They were expanding the school in its new premises at Newbury in Berkshire, having moved from Burgess Hill in Sussex.

Mother now went *out* to work. She found it a pleasure, revelling in her new-found *freedom!* Father had to *toe the line a bit now*. He still had a rotten tongue and used it on us all except the three little ones. Every other word was almost always the F word. He seemed never able to say a sentence without the F word. Today that word makes me *cringe* and go *cold* all over. Father stayed home, literally bandaging himself with gauze, bandages, creams and potions – his hands, his arms, his legs and sometimes his face. It was a dreadful disease. It did not improve his temper one iota! Mother did various jobs, including Christmas postwoman and working in a laundry. She fetched home unmarked *lost handkerchiefs*, over which we argued about who was going to have the prettiest. Mother used to say, "Quit yers 'ollerin' or yers won't get any next munf!"

Before my illness, which robbed me of normal hearing, Mother used to give each of us a halfpenny to buy a carrot to eat on our way to Grafton Road Primary and Junior School. It was great for our teeth! We had good teeth. I still have twenty-two of my own teeth. Up to the year before her death our mother still had twelve of her own teeth. A few were removed at the London Hospital dental section some time before her death.

She used to clean them with soot during the war and then with a tin of dentifrice afterwards, when war ended.

My life in England was certainly different from my Welsh life, where I was cossetted and greatly loved and I suppose *spoilt in a nice way*.

Our mother in England used to *stitch us* into our clothes – literally, especially in wintertime. If a button was missing and another one couldn't be found to fit the hole Mother got some strong cotton, and after several attempts to thread the needle we'd do it for her. She then stitched the garment with a few stitches and at night just snipped the cotton so we could undress! This was quite a novelty to me, but the norm to my sisters! Even when she went out to work Mother still had the washing and cooking to do for us. The cleaning and shopping was done by us girls.

All his life Father seemed to be in and out of hospital with pleurisy and bronchitis and similar ailments to do with his breathing – including asthma later on. The ambulance was always rushing to 48 with its ting-a-ling noise and picking up Father and screeching off full blast to Oldchurch Hospital. He was in there so many times he could have qualified as a member of the staff! At least he had passed his first-aid course in the ARP (air-raid precautions).

The girls often took a single bed downstairs for him, then took it back upstairs again! In later life he had glaucoma, a hearing aid and a pacemaker. Father seemed almost immortal (so Matilda said)! Our mother must have been one of the best *home nurses* ever – unpaid, of course. I often muse about how much money she'd saved the NHS by taking care of Father in between going out to work. Mother's last working years included a lengthy time working for Ever Ready batteries. Everyday she stuck and wound brown sticky paper on the ends of her fingers, which helped prevent them being cut by the sharp metal of the empty batteries.

Mother was always *boiling something*: boiling the potato peelings for the bran mash for the chickens; boiling and then simmering her wonderful stews, which had a taste all of their very own; boiling the white handkerchiefs which Father was always spitting phlegm into; boiling for the older girls the white rags used when they had Eve's curse each month. That was before sanitary towels were reasonably priced and available. At Mary Hare Grammar School we were boarders and girls had free sanitary pads.

Contrary to what you may be thinking, Father did not always *look* ill. He was a *picture* of health with a short stocky build and barrel-shaped chest. And he kept his head of hair all his life!

Having been raised in Wales since the age of four, I did not know him and when I remet him I did not like him. It was probably mutual. I was capable of standing my ground and having my say. I knew home life did not have to consist of bullying and the F word every time he had something to say. Father was apt to play one daughter off against the other – like chess! *We all got on well together otherwise.* We cottoned on to Father's little lark and decided what he didn't know wouldn't hurt him. Whoever was spending the most money on Father each week was *the* flavour of the week or day. He could be an awkward cuss, could Father. Mind you, with all those knitting needles clicking away in that small room where we ate, socialised and *made our faces up* in the large mirror over the mantelshelf, it was enough to give anyone a *headache*, I'm sure. For our part it was a relief for us there was no little Albert following in his *not so good* footsteps.

He would never hear a word against Emmie after she went to live in America. Neither would we girls – we loved her all our lives.

Our parents *wanted for nothing*. They crossed the pond to the USA umpteen times. Their longest stay was six months. They came home loaded up with gifts, including clothes and jewellery. Mother's box room at *48* was like Aladdin's cave. Even she could not recall what exactly was in that room, unused or unworn. Before Mother died she gave me her little pillbox hat. Emmie's son had shot a pheasant and Emmie had the feathered hat made. I am the only *girl* who now wears hats. I love hats. The newspaper at the bottom of the hatbox was over thirty years old!

Matilda lost count of the pairs of gold earrings she purchased for Mother.

Eileen paid for the phone to be installed at *48*. Emmie now called over the phone from the USA. They loved her calls.

I made some of Mother's clothes for her: the black dress with gold trimming she wore at her golden wedding was made by me; I also made mine.

Emmie had them live six months in a trailer on her land to see if they'd like to stay for good. They wanted to go home eventually at the end of the trial (homesick). They loved the USA for a holiday, but not to live there permanently. Our parents went to many musicals and other shows – again paid for and arranged by one or more of us girls. For fourteen years Doreen and her husband paid their bills – gas and electricity – quarterly.

Matilda is a trained confectioner and made all the celebration cakes, including the golden-wedding cake and the welcome-home cake for Queenie from Australia and the girls from America – a double occasion. *Fortunately* for us, Father was taken bad with pleurisy or bronchitis. The *foreign* girls went to see him in hospital. Father told the men and nurses about his ten daughters.

At *48* at weekends Mother was a commander-in-chief! You'd hear her call out the orders of the day. It was safer to obey than to be a *dissident*. Emily obviously believed the old adage '*The devil makes work for idle hands*'! Mother's voice carried. "Clean the kitchen, Vilie [me]. Get up them stairs. Here's a nice drop of mixed vinegar and warm water. Polish the mahogany bedroom suite with it. Use it sparingly. Use this soft cloth to rub it down to a nice shine. Plenty of elbow grease, my young lady! Wash them dishes an' put them away carefully. Queenie, Eileen, get yer coats on. Catch a bus ter Green Lanes. 'Ere's the coppers for yer fares. Oh! Yer've got some coppers already. Well, you don't need mine, then." Hers went back into her purse. "Now mind youse gets the sausages from Sainsbury's. Albert only likes theirs! 'E'll 'oller youse back out the door iffen youse comes back wiv anyfink else! Make sure yer gets Cox's apples. I like them best. Get some mild Cheddar cheese, 'n' make sure the girl on the butter counter *pats off* a nice bit of Anchor butter on to the scales. If it's not quite enough, make 'er add on a bit extra. Likes *me* cheese wiv cream crackers, I duz."

Way above Mother's voice we could hear the milkman yodelling out, "*Milkkkkkooooooooo!*"

"Here's *them* there ration books. Don't forget ter count yer change. Make sure they don't mark the wrong coupons like last week – silly b—! Come on, girls! We ain't got *orl day*!" Mother opened the front door to usher the girls out. She cocked an ear. "'Ark, that's the milkman. Sounds like 'e's in Winifred Road. One minute – yes, 'e is. Where's me purse?"

"In yer 'and," sighed Eileen.

Mother cackled loudly, "Oh yerse, it is. Silly me! Vilie [hollering up the stairs to me], come down 'ere 'n' get ready ter pay the milkman! Me cuppa tea's gettin' cold. Off youse goes, girls. Watch yer change." (My sister told me this.)

All the while Father would sit at the table reading his daily rag (newspaper), mouthing to himself sotto voce. Father left school at eleven, but he could read and write. His writing did scrawl, but after a while you got to *read it*. He couldn't spell very well, hence the words tailing off. But he was more literate and numerate than many modern school-leavers after eleven years of schooling! Mother always drank her tea from the saucer. Pouring a drop from her cup, she artistically crooked her fingers with the *pinkie* sticking forward and sipped from the saucer. It was very dainty! No matter who was there or not Emily drank like that – always.

In later years, when I went to afternoon tea with Lady E. M. Templar, wife of Field Marshal Sir Gerald Templar, at their many-storeyed house in London I noticed she held her cup in *both hands* and not by the handle. I mentioned it to her as we were chatting and she said it was a habit from years of living in a Commonwealth country. Then I told her how Mother held her saucer. She thought that was delightful.

Mother having done a lot of washing and the girls home again, she checked the groceries and pronounced herself satisfied. In those days she knew the price down to the last farthing. We all did. The girls had bought her a bunch of flowers or a little *something*. She used to thank them warmly.

Father asleep with his head on the table would raise it, smile and say, "Oh, ain't that nice!" then drop his head and be fast asleep again.

My sisters were very attractive girls and great fun to be with once I got to know them. They were always washing and fixing each other's hair, all smoking! I hated the smoke. Our parents smoked and the boyfriends did too, all in our little kitchen-cum-living room. There were two armchairs and we girls sat on ordinary wooden chairs all in a row round the room. We mostly sat with one leg folded under us, playing cards, telling jokes and chatting incessantly. It was a very companionable way of life, as different from my time in Wales as chalk is from cheese. The girls taught me all the songs and jitterbugged with me! I learnt 'The Knock-Kneed Jig' in an office I worked in (a later one), and we did it at *48* to the record blaring out:

> 'I'm a bow-legged chicken, I'm a knock-kneed hen,
> Never been so happy since I don't know when. . . .'

I had never done so much singing in my life outside of chapel on Sundays in Wales. It was great fun. We were a noisy laughing *lot*. I wonder in retrospect how Father kept his sanity. I mean all his daughters and their girlfriends and some of the boyfriends would be there. The kitchenette (scullery) and the hallway right up to the front door was always packed with bodies. (Our living room was about twelve feet by twelve feet!)

Emmie used to ring from America and everyone wanted to speak to her all together. *It was crazy at 48 sometimes*. But we were happy. We made our own happiness together. Mother really was a clean woman. Even the gas cooker had to be pulled forward and cleaned behind quite often!

Emmie living in America had two children. Harold was a salesman and he had the gift of the gab. He invested his money and did so well he was able to quit work at least ten years or more before retirement age. They had thirty-three acres of land and had pinto horses.

When Greg, their only son, was twenty he was killed in an explosion in Richmond, Indiana (under a gun shop). They found his body on the Sunday in the basement of a beauty parlour – blown there. Many people were killed. It was horrendous. Greg was attending Purdue University, training as a vet. He was a pinto horse judge and always wore cowboy clothes – a lovely lad. He'd been deferred from Vietnam as he still had to finish his course. His body is buried with all his mates and school friends in the same cemetery. They were brought back from the Vietnam War in body bags. It is still painful to think about it. His poor parents and sister never really got over it. Their daughter won many awards as a horsewoman. God blessed her with three sons – Emmie's pride and joy.

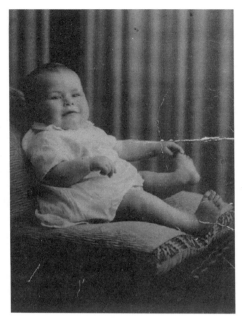

Violet aged six months.

Violet just turned eighteen (1954).   *Violet aged eight and a half (1944).*

Our parents and eight of their ten daughters, 1947. Back row, second left is Violet, just gone deaf three months previously. This photo was sent to Emmie in the USA, as she asked for it.

Violet on Alice's lap on the doorstep of 1 Rock Cottages.

*Violet's Welsh foster-parents, Alice and Bill Onions,
on their wedding day, 1939.*

*1 Rock Cottages, Blackwood, South Wales. This is the cottage Violet
lived in during the Second World War. This is Alice's son Colin, born in
1946. The cottage is now part of The Rock Inn.*

Emily (Emmie) aged about twenty or twenty-one with her first two daughters, Emmie and Matilda.

Fellow evacuee Maureen, who came to live with Violet.

The marriage of Esther Jenkins to Wilfred. Violet is standing front left next to Winnie.

Hop picking in Sussex, 1950. Back row: Harry holding baby Joan, Doreen in front of pole. Front row: Harry's sister Annie, Mary, Emily in bib and brace trousers, Mrs Edwards, Marie and Albert.

Sister Emmie with her fiancé, Harold, from Indiana, USA, on their engagement day in wartime England, 1944. They were married from 1945 to 1999.

Emily and Albert with Emmie next to him. Eileen is next to Tiny, who is sitting on the stool. Photo taken after Thelma's funeral.

The Old Summer House at Mary Hare Grammar School, Arlington Manor.

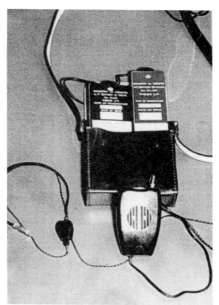

Photo courtesy of the Royal National Institute for the Deaf Library.
A 1948–fifties era NHS body-worn hearing aid. The band on the left,
worn over the head, was for bone conduction. The author did not wear
this band. She had an ear insert for her hearing aid.
The batteries were quite heavy.

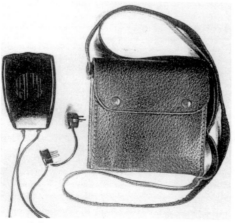

Photo courtesy of the Royal National Institute for the Deaf Library.
A microphone and earpiece insert (not shown) and bag containing the
batteries of the NHS hearing aid the author wore in the 1948–fifties era.
The leather bag and strap were slung across the chest; the microphone
was clipped to the strap.

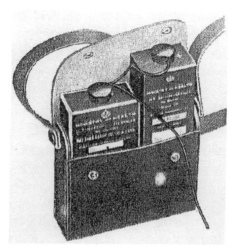

I do not want anyone who might be able to take advantage of the service not to do so because they might be called upon to meet some expense in connection with the replenishment of the batteries of the hearing aid. Therefore, we decided to have a battery which is large enough to last a reasonable space of time and would not, therefore, have to be replenished too often. So we have made this compromise, and like every compromise in this world it is not perfect, but we believe it is effective and efficient.

Photo courtesy of the Royal National Institute for the Deaf Library.
A 1948–fifties era NHS body-worn hearing aid.

Emily's sister Auntie Ada Bird, 'our Mary' and Emily strawberry
picking in Wisbech.

Violet outside 48 Gerald Road in her boarding-school Girl Guide uniform.

Gregory, only son of Emmie and Harold. Born 1948; killed 1968.

Teacher Miss Mabel Brink and headmistress Miss V. Kathleen Mitchell from the West Ham School for the Deaf, 1949.

The Mary Hare Grammar School for the Deaf, Arlington Manor, Newbury, Berkshire, 1950.

The pupils, principal and staff at Mary Hare Grammar School, early 1950s. Violet is standing on the extreme left of the second row from the top.

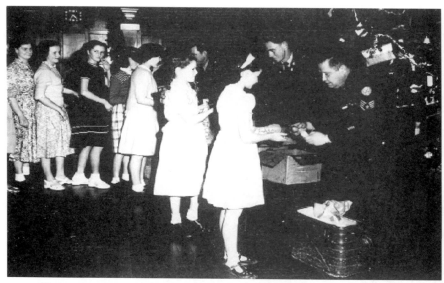

Christmas party at Mary Hare Grammar School, 1951, with American servicemen as guests. Left to right: Jean, Pam, Elaine, Joan, Rosa, Jennifer and Anne.

Old school photo – PE lesson. Back row: Joan, Anne-Marie, Pat, Mr Ainge, Violet, Jeanne, Cyrilla, Angela. Middle row: Jean, Eileen, Nora, Audrey, Joan, Jean. Front row: Ena, Dorothy, Irene.

Sitting amongst the daffodils at Mary Hare Grammar School. Left to right: Joan, Ruth, Elaine, Rosalia.

One of the school's football teams in the 1950s.
The strip was green and white.

Mary Hare Grammar School, 1950 group. Violet is in the second row
from the bottom, third from the right.

Violet in school uniform.

The Mary Hare Grammar School's Girl Guide troop. Violet was in Kingfisher Patrol. She is fifth from the right of this guard of honour for Princess Margaret, the school's patron, 1951.

No. 82/525

London and Home Counties
Regional Advisory Council for Technological Education

This is to certify that

Mrs Vie FOOT

attended an approved STAGE I course of training
for part-time teachers of Adult Education
and satisfied the requirements
of the course

M.G. Venn .

Chairman of the Council

Director

G Russell

Convenor
N E Sector Board

*An extra qualification in 1982: Violet teaching communication skills
and lecturing on deafness to hearing people.*

*Old school reunion photo: Derek, Anne-Marie, Billy, Rosalind, David
W., Violet and Alan at a reunion in London.*

A school sports day, St John of Beverley (yellow) House: boys and girls marching together.

Violet at Stratford-upon-Avon.

Guard of honour for Princess Margaret, the school's patron, at Mary Hare Grammar School, 1951. The Princess wore blush pink. Violet is the eighth female from the left of the Girl Guides. Boy Scouts from the school made up the rest of the guard of honour. Mr Askew, the principal, is in his robes.

Old school photo of Jean Smith and Violet. The Beekeeping Club at school sold the honey to the school.

Violet, back row far left with seven of her nine sisters, 1973.

The only known photo of Emily with all nine of her ten living daughters.

Six Old Hares at Violet's eightieth birthday. Back row, Desmond, husband of Elaine, Donald B. and Ronald S. Front row, Elaine B., Rosa B., Violet, Jennifer M. and Terri (Ronald's wife).

Emily (Emmie) Humphreys aged sixty-six and her grandchildren, 1973 or 1974. Robbie Foot is in a striped-sleeved jumper.

Brighton reunion: are all ex-MHGS pupils Violet knew in 1949–53.

The conservatory, MHGS, 1986, Rosalind, Jeanne, Violet and Cyrilla.

*Violet's beloved Second World War Welsh foster-parents (1940–1945),
Alice and Bill Onions.*

Violet's wonderful sons, Robert and James, 1968.

Mary, Tony B., Elaine L., Rosa R., Jean S., Jeanne hiding behind Violet,
Audrey S. and Eleanor H. – reunion at Brighton of ex-MHGS pupils.

MHGS old pupils' holiday in Dorset.
Violet with sticks, Anne wearing dark trousers.

Violet and her late husband, Fred, off to a school reunion at a London hotel for a banquet and ballroom dancing.

Our mother, Emily, sixty-six years old. Golden wedding anniversary. Violet made her frock.

Dinner and Dance reunion MHGS, including Ralph Hawley, Ralph Drewry, June Fielding, Jean and Donald. An old slide from over forty years ago, printed 2010. Violet in the white dress.

Violet's grandchildren Christopher Mark, Charlotte Marie Elizabeth and Ashley Benjamin. Children of son Robert and Caroline.

Violet's grandsons, sons of James and Barbara, Matthew and Wesley.

Violet with one son, four grandsons, four great-grandsons and one great-granddaughter.

Audrey Sutton (née Pettifer) and Violet, Hotel Brighton, MHGS reunion, 1996. Audrey was ill with Pick's disease.

Joan Evelyn Middleton, sister Tiny's only living child, made her own clothes for a Civil War re-enactment they took part in. Joan was a Justice of the Peace for twenty years.

MHGS old pupil Rosa Robb – lovely pic of her.

Matilda and Harry's granddaughter, Helen Rose, PhD (physics and planetary sciences), working in the space industry.

Doreen's children (she had seven, one died at birth) –
Violet's nephews and nieces.

MHGS reunion at Arlington Manor. Sitting, Ann R., Jenny M., Violet
and Valerie W.; standing, Ruth G., Mary M. and David M.

Violet with her first great-grandchild, Eleanor, 2015.

In a hotel. Rosa Robb, Violet and Jean Sellers (née Baker, Humphreys and Goadsby, from the same school).

Violet's son Robert laughing his head off at her sister Ada's son Keith.

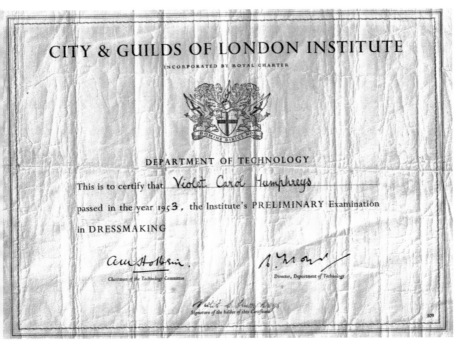

Violet's Certificate of Dressmaking, 1953.

Violet's time-consuming crewel work of Jeremy Fisher took her ages to stitch – one of her finest works.

ASSOCIATED EXAMINING BOARD

GENERAL CERTIFICATE OF EDUCATION

This is to certify that   VIOLET CAROL FOOT

born   24   DECEMBER   1935

sat for the General Certificate of Education
at
EAST HAM TECHNICAL COLLEGE

and reached pass standard in the following subject(s) in May/June 1968

ORDINARY   LEVEL

IN   1   SUBJECT(S)

ECONOMIC AND SOCIAL HISTORY

*   *   *   *   *   *   *   *

Signed on behalf of the Associated Examining Board

B. C. Lucia.

Secretary to the Board

THE DEPARTMENT OF EDUCATION AND SCIENCE ACCEPTS THE EXAMINATION
AS REACHING THE APPROVED STANDARD

Signed on behalf of the Department of Education and Science

Under-Secretary

*Violet took the daytime course to see if she could cope without any
helpers. It was hard going, especially when tutors walked up and down.*

UNIVERSITY OF OXFORD

DELEGACY OF LOCAL EXAMINATIONS

GENERAL CERTIFICATE OF EDUCATION

This is to certify that, in the examination held in Summer 1953,

Violet Carol Humphreys

born the 24th *day of* December *in the year* 1935
reached the Pass Standard at Ordinary Level in the following four
subjects:—

English Language

English Literature (Selected)

History (British)

Art

Signed on behalf of the above-named examining body

CENTRE AND INDEX NUMBER:
Arlington Manor 9

VICE-CHANCELLOR OF OXFORD UNIVERSITY

THE MINISTRY OF EDUCATION *accepts the examination as reaching
the approved standard.*

Signed on behalf of the Ministry of Education

*Violet's O-level certificate, English Language,
English Literature, History (British) and Art as marked by
Oxford University professionals, 1953.*

THE ROYAL NATIONAL INSTITUTE
FOR THE DEAF

105 GOWER STREET, LONDON, WC1E 6AH

No. 1 – DECEMBER 1970.

THIS IS TO CERTIFY THAT

VIOLET CAROL FOOT

has satisfied

The Examining Board

of the City Literary Institute

as to her competency to teach

Lipreading to Deaf or Deafened persons

over school leaving age

_____ *Chairman*

_____ *Secretary-General*

_____ *Principal*
The City Literary Institute

THIS CERTIFICATE DOES NOT QUALIFY THE HOLDER TO TEACH LIP-READING TO CHILDREN UNDER SCHOOL LEAVING AGE

Violet's certificate, the No. 1, to pass as a lipreading tutor.

Half-Yearly Progress Report

Pupil's Name ......HUMPHREYS....Violet...... Date............................

Age: ...17..yrs. ...0....mths. Form..VA.........

L.E.A...Essex.C.C...

1. SCHOOL WORK — Assessed on ABCDE Scale.

SUBJECT.	Estimate.	
Speech	A –	NVS
Lipreading	C –	NVS
English Language	B	S
English Literature	C+	
French		
Latin		
History	B	Ab
Geography		
Citizenship		
Religious Knowledge	C	EB
General Mathematics		
Arithmetic		
General Science		
Domestic Science		
Needlework		
Art	B	NVS
Wood/Metal Work		
Games and P.T.	C –	KH.
Swimming		
Special Subjects	Extra Mural - Dressmaking	

2. SPECIAL ABILITIES AND INTERESTS Industrious & valued member of School Library Committee. Dancing Dressmaking

3. TEMPERAMENTAL QUALITIES AND CONDUCT Always ready to help others.

4. HEALTH:
Height 5' 1½" Weight 10st 12lb 2oz General Condition A:............
Health good.
Attendance Regular.
Special Treatment nil

5. REMARKS ON GENERAL PROGRESS: Has worked hard and made steady progress
Most helpful & cooperative.

Violet's end of term report. Mr Askew, the principal, wrote on the bottom, 'Most helpful and cooperative.'

CHAPTER TEN

At one time, after I was married, Albert decided to get a flat-back lorry, stocking it with vegetables. Our mother, Emily, in a crisp whiter-than-white overall sat gaily on the tailboard as Albert drove from street to street. Mother weighed the vegetables on the big weighing scales and Father did his best costermonger voice.

After a time that palled and they gave it up. Father then bought a *mods-and-rockers*-style scooter, scootering around the streets with Mother perched bravely behind him.

Mother could make you the best egg and chips you've ever eaten or the best piece of fish in batter (fried). To skin a flat plaice Mother put a clean tea towel at the end of it. Gripping it in her mouth – hey presto! – she pulled the skin off as neat as could be.

I doubt if Father's vegetables were covered in pesticides as many are undoubtedly today. They were grown in our back garden and he relied on bonemeal.

To see Mother's girls getting togged up just to go to see friends or family or shopping was a sight for sore eyes. Our hair was curled with metal Dinkie curlers. There were no rollers or modern hairsprays. We used Amami wave setting lotion and metal tongs heated on the gas flame. The house took on the appearance of a hairdressing salon. Our bouffant paper nylon petticoats were stiffened with a mixture of sugar and water! The Christian Dior look arrived and was greeted enthusiastically by women and girls starved of new clothing for six long years of war.

Ecstatic, we saved and bought a very best dress and made a very best half-slip. We had one best dress, one half-slip, one skirt and two or three blouses. We knitted our own jumpers and cardigans. We also had one pair of best stiletto heels and one pair of flat shoes. That was the extent of our personal wardrobes. (We didn't

actually have wardrobes; we hung them from the bedroom door.)
Only Mother and Father had wardrobes.

Just to go shopping we wore our best short nylon gloves, in
different colours to match our nylons, which now appeared. I
used to love my lavender stockings and matching nylon gloves.
As we sashayed along Gerald Road with our fancy half-slips
flouncing up and down under the billowing skirt half of our
dresses we were the bee's knees! Yes! The stiletto shoes hurt,
especially when winkle-pickers came into vogue! What did it
matter as long as we *looked feminine and sexy*! Sex was not so
blatant and open in those days, nor spoken about. It was the *New
Look* and the whole outfit which gave us *our thrills*!

People not used to the drabness of the war years, the poverty
prevailing and fewer goods, perhaps would not understand the
excessive joy we culled from the *whole* of our ensembles. Going
upstairs on the buses gave a thrill to the men following behind
us! Not that they saw much – just our half-slips! But imagination
sometimes works better for men rather than the whole caboodle
of *sex on a dish*.

At *48* Father would be muttering to himself about something
in the day's copy of the *Daily Mirror*.

The girls came home with the latest record released. We'd
all join in singing, whether it was Frankie Laine, Perry Como,
Dickie Valentine, Donald Peers or Lonnie Donegan. Great fun!
We practically ate and breathed music at *48*, from 'Catch a
Falling Star' to 'She Wears Red Feathers and a Hula Hula Skirt'
to 'In a Shady Nook by a Babbling Brook' to' Standing on the
Corner Watching All the Girls Go By'.

To the returned prodigal from Wales my siblings were love
and kindness itself. I cannot remember rowing with any of them
actually. After I became deaf, of course it was more difficult for
them. I had no hearing aid. I used to wonder what jokes they were
laughing about on the radio. By the time they'd patiently related it
to me they had rudely missed another three or four jokes. Anyway,
the jokes related from their mouths were not as funny as they *heard
them* on the radio. The time of silence began in December 1946!

It was another cold day, with Mr Frosty making pretty pictures
on the inside and outside of the bedroom windows. We had no
central heating and I didn't know any house which did. It was
the month of my eleventh birthday, 24 December. There were
still some weeks to go yet, with Christmas Day and Boxing Day

following it, the latter being when in the old days apprentices of medieval times or some such date were given their yearly *present* from their boss. The money was inside a sealed box and the box had to be ceremoniously broken open by the young lads. It was a great day in their lives, for they worked for a pittance until they were time-served craftsmen or whatever.

Emmie told us they did not have Boxing Day in America and people only had one day off: Christmas Day. Obviously Boxing Day was not taken to the Americas with the Pilgrim Fathers on the *Mayflower*.

I had returned from South Wales to the land of my ancestors in excellent health. Plump and hale-looking, I could not recall ever suffering from headaches, taking everything life threw at me in my stride.

That particular day is etched forever in my memory cells. I was attending junior school at Grafton Road, and looking forward to entering the *big school* at Tenterden Road sometime in the following year.

Most things happen to me on a Tuesday and this was no exception. I suddenly had a terrible headache, and my neck and back arched back like a bow with a taut string ready to loosen the arrow at its target. I got home with the help of my little sisters. Later when the doctor came he took one look from the doorway! "Meningitis!" he pronounced. He might just as well have said, "*The plague.*" The horror struck into the hearts and minds of our family. They knew it was a BIG killer then (and still is today). Emily thought my death warrant had been signed!

The ambulance was called and I was rushed to Romford Isolation Hospital. My hitherto ordinary day had taken an unexpected twist that *changed my life for ever.*

First it was to Wales and a foster-family; *now* it was the time of the *big silence*. God certainly moves in mysterious ways His wonders to perform.

I do not ever look back with regret on that point. The rest of my life, so far, has been very interesting and remunerative, in terms of my own husband and children and grandchildren. *Good often comes from bad if we look for the silver lining.* Being young, knowing nothing about deafness, nor having heard the word, and not actually having met a deaf person, I was in ignorance of my fate. I probably did feel sorry for myself at this dreadful predicament. I possibly cried a lot of tears. I may have shouted (and I think I did), "Why me? Why not Emmie, Matilda, Eileen or Queenie? Why me?"

This was quite a logical way to look at it after I recovered.

I adore music, and it was during a music lesson at school. Whether it was just an impromptu class *happening* or a proper lesson I do not recall. I do know the music scales were chalked on the blackboard by the teacher. She drew a nice staircase and on each step she placed a note: doh, ray, me, fah, soh, lah, te, doh. Up that staircase we kept *singing*, then we graduated to the down staircase, reversing the notes. When she was satisfied we'd got the hang of it we were *importantly* permitted to go up the scales and down in perfect order and harmony. Our teacher was most pleased with us. Placing her *baton* under her arm she gave us all a big clap.

Never having suffered from headaches I was surprised to gradually find my head *bothering me*. I felt dreadful physically, and puzzled too. The notes from the piano tinkled in my head and I felt *all muddled* in my thinking. I love the sound of a piano playing, and I was a bit peeved that my enjoyment *that morning* was being superseded by this nasty old pain in my head, neck and back.

Verdict: TB cerebrospinal meningitis. I was put into an isolation cubicle in Romford Isolation Hospital, Essex, with curtains drawn behind the glass of the next cubicle and mine. Father and Mother had to don white coats and white masks to come into my *room*. Anything given to me had to be sterilised first. Father brought some eggs from his chickens with my name on them in pencil (they were not sterilised). Nurse took them away. Rationing was still in force, but I don't think eggs were still rationed. The hospital wanted to operate to relieve the pressure on my brain, but Father refused to countenance it, fearing worse damage of the brain. Even today I still get pressure there behind my eyes – especially the right eye. It is kept monitored twice a year by my optician and the hospital eye specialist. I now have glaucoma in both eyes.

I assumed, in my innocence, that I would recover and be *myself* again in due course. One went into hospital to *get better* – everyone knew that! I did not notice at first the loss of hearing! I saw my parents in their masks and pity in their eyes. I did wonder why they never spoke to me. (They did!) In my little *new world* I was cocooned.

One day Nurse came breezing in and I did not know what she was saying and the penny dropped! I screamed blue murder! I was probably thinking they'd removed my hearing because I was poorly. I wanted them to give it back to me! I screamed at Nurse, working myself up into a *tizzy*, "I can't hear you!"

Nurse hurriedly gave me a drink of something and I in my innocence (we were innocent in those days – no televisions showing medical programmes!) fell fast asleep.

Christmas Day dawned and I sat up in bed, still in the glass-walled room. Curtains were drawn over the glass walls. Nurse bathed me all over and did my hair with a pretty bow. Father Christmas appeared, but did not actually *enter* my room. He waved and gave Nurse a present for me, waiting till I opened it. It was nice – a felt bag made by someone in Australia from a women's institute. I waved to Father Christmas. I did not know what he said, but he opened and shut his mouth a few times, pointing to the bag. He wanted me to open it. I did and took out a blue felt mouse with a very long rolled blue felt tail! That made me grin. Father Christmas clasped his two hands together and shook them above his head like a triumphant boxer! He was nice. The handbag and mouse never left the hospital with me!

Another day Nurse came in and pointed to the glass between me and the next isolation cubicle. A young lady in bed held up a brand new baby. Its mouth was open and its face all screwed up. My jolly little nurse gestured to the baby and drew a forefinger slowly down one cheek: the baby was crying! I got the *silent* message OK. After I'd waved and nodded my head the curtain was swished closed in the other glass cubicle. I did wonder what a baby was doing in an isolation ward. The mother was tucked into the bed; presumably she'd also got an *isolation* condition.

In January I was given a *special* injection. My family tell me it was streptomycin, newly arrived from America. This was 1947. I'd gone into hospital at ten and came out later at eleven years old. My second Christmas in England since I was a toddler was not spent with my siblings, but in an isolation room! Life was beginning its twists and turns *and I was now deaf.* Eventually my sister Matilda slipped into my room to make sure I was OK! Working as a maid in the nurses' house/section, she was present without permission. Matilda got a very stiff rollicking from authority.

I will gloss over this part of my life. It is still a very painful memory.

Matilda took me home on the bus. Because the hospital said I had to walk as much as possible, poor Matilda, at four feet eleven inches, had to help home this awful thin staggering bewildered child who was now deaf!

We fell about laughing as I dragged her sideways and north, south, east and west. My balance was terribly poor and is not much better today! On the bus the conductor made a fuss of me; so did a few passengers, who gave me sweets. They were strangers. I expect Matilda apologised for my *staggering* aboard because I'd gone deaf! They meant well. With all their silent mouths opening and shutting I could have been forgiven if I had thought I was on another planet! We didn't think about that kind of thing (planets) then.

Nobody in hospital had actually told me I was permanently deaf. It was assumed that ignorance is bliss in our time. Matilda had been told to *make* me walk to the bus, *make* me clamber on to the platform and chat to me as if I was *normal* even though I did not know what she was saying. Thus was my rude introduction to the art of lip-reading coupled with expansive gestures and facial grimaces!

Oh dearie me! As far as I was concerned I was *normal*! I sometimes think there is no such thing as *normal* in life. We are all different; what is *normal* to one is not to another. Tricky word for definition – normal!

The penny had dropped whilst I was still in my cubicle *room*. In my innocence I assumed that time would make my ears grow back! Such is life's effort to cling to any straw.

I don't think I was particularly brave! I didn't have much choice. I was deaf and that was that. All the tears in the world would not alter that fact. 'Sufficient unto the day' was how I looked at life. *Mañana!* I'd survived being *ripped* from my *parents and siblings* being *fostered* until I was nine and a half, being *ripped* from my *foster-parents* and returned to an unknown large family. *And within less than two years I'd entered the world of silence!* Quite a journey in one of tender years! Children were expected to be seen and not heard and there was no *counselling* for me. One only needed to know *what's what and when's when* on a daily basis.

It was not until my adult years that Matilda told me she'd got into hot water for entering an isolation cubicle room. Matilda said, "We survived the horrors of the war and the Blitz, which killed 30,000 people in London, and elsewhere another 11,000; I wasn't going to let this meningitis thing keep me from my little sister."

Before leaving hospital that day the nurses got me on to my

feet over the weeks and I bowled them over like ninepins. My legs went one way, my body another. The staff worked hard on my locomotion! It was imperative to learn to walk and balance myself and get back into the *normal world*. Not an easy task! One learns to walk as a toddler; then I had to *relearn* again as an eleven-year-old; and I had to relearn *again* after multiple sclerosis later in life. Life seemed to me to consist of one learning process after another. It has given a *fizz* to life, wondering what the next challenge will be.

I may not have had the pleasure of all the things which have happened to me (and the family I have of my own) if I had not had meningitis and gone deaf!

I would not have met my beloved husband and maybe not gone to my wonderful grammar school. The list of *maybe*s is endless! Life is never a bowl of cherries. There has to be pips along the way. It is a measure of our character that we face these *difficulties and happenings* head on and strive to make the best of the hand of cards which we have been dealt. No, it is not a *picnic*, but always worthwhile eventually.

I had missed Christmas at home with my sisters. It was now the end of January 1947. Mother was kneeling on the floor taking the ash pan from the fireplace. I said, "Hello, Mum. I can't hear properly yet, but I will tomorrow!"

Mother burst into tears, and throwing her apron over her face she rushed from the room leaving me standing there *in ignorance*. They do say that *ignorance is bliss*. At that moment it must have been *very blissful* for me!

Father armed himself with a piece of paper and a well-sharpened pencil and proceeded to write things down for me when people spoke, like 'Mother says would you like something to eat?' and other innocuous things of no particular importance. People – and there were many in the house (*visiting*, not just our family) – preferred to sit and *stare* at the new *deaf-and-dumb* girl! I was far from dumb had they but known it! But deaf was linked with *dumb* in a horrid way. I therefore became '*poor Emily's* deaf-and-dumb daughter' – an object to fear and pity. They knew no different, and neither did the rest of the hoi polloi of our world. I was not stone deaf; I could hear some sounds (mainly low ones – the high ones had gone) if they shouted into my right ear. The amount left in the left ear was not known until a long time later when NHS hearing aids were available. It was negligible and soon gone. Later, when hearing aids became available free it was not possible to use one in the left ear, only the right one. Today the left ear has no feeling at all – you could push a knitting needle into it! I could sometimes distinguish (from shouting in my right ear) vowel sounds, but not consonants. So a word like book would to me be "-oo-" and half would be "-ah-". The rest had to be guessed! Communication became a great strain on me and the nerves of my family. Consonants, like p, b, m, k, l, r, sh, zh and so on, had *kissed me goodbye*!

How silly everyone looked, and the number of neighbours who found *excuses* to call in on Emily AND HER DEAF-AND-DUMB DAUGHTER! Their mouths would open and shut like goldfish. I had a job to keep a straight face! It would have been most impolite and improper to have told them of the similarity! Besides, children were to be seen and not heard! They could not invade the secrecy of my mind and thoughts, which was a small crumb of satisfactory comfort in my *new world of silence*.

Still nobody explained deafness to me!

About a month or so later an erstwhile local friend called and asked me to go out and play the 'Kokerrooshah' game. I don't know how it is spelt, and neither does anyone else as far as I am aware! You had to hop on one foot with your arms folded across your chest and charge everyone else! The object was to knock an opponent off balance so their bent leg, or rather the foot of their bent leg, touched the ground as you charged them. Some children were quite skilled in keeping their balance.

Mother shook her head and said I could not go out because I was too weak. Feeling a *rebellious little Violet*, I disobeyed and out I went – just in the road outside *48*! Of course I could not balance on two legs, let alone one and hop too! The edge of the kerb rose to meet me and the lamp post refused to hold me steady. Stars literally twinkled in my poor old head! My face smashed into the kerb edge, and my front teeth actually went through my bottom lip. I bear the scar today. An ambulance was called and off I was rushed to St George's Hospital, Seven Kings, to return home bandaged like the Invisible Man. There was no spare bed for me at *48*, so Father brought down from the loft the huge iron cradle! And there I slept, all eleven years of me, sipping liquids through a straw, and my mouth was terribly painful.

Oh, the pity of deafness! Oh, the frustration! Anger – every emotion possible – entered my *new life*. An inferiority complex set in: everybody seemed to be talking about *me*. I did not know anything about lip-reading; neither did any of our family friends or neighbours. I did not know sign language; neither did they. Oh the *pity, pity, pity* in people's faces. I loathed it. My sisters were wonderful, *keeping me in the picture* by hook or by crook.

I was never allowed out of the front gate on my own! Never to go anywhere alone! I had to be *chaperoned* for safety's sake! Out shopping, my sisters would obediently obey Mother, hollering out, "Grab hold of Violet." The first I knew of it was one or more of them clutching the back of my clothing (like a toddler) when we crossed roads.

I became haughty, bad-tempered, with a thick Welsh accent. My memory banks had retained my Welsh accent and way of speaking for I had only been back in England since May 1945 and it was now the end of January 1947 – not quite *two* years, more or less.

Previously of a sunny disposition, I retired into a shell of my own making and became inward-looking: it was a *safe cop out*! No professionals called to tell me about deafness. There were many worse sorrows and troubles in the world following the aftermath and consequences of the Second World War. There were many millions of displaced persons and refugees at home and abroad. *Pity* became a very overworked word as a result of the war. Meningitis was quite prevalent in 1946! My Welsh accent and my deafness made me *different* at *48*. The only books in our house were *Film Star Annual*s and magazines like *Red Letter* and *Picture Post*; the latter was a great favourite in wartime and peace, sadly mourned at its eventual demise in later years. I retreated into my own *private* world, reading and rereading them over and over again. Nobody disturbed me. Mother even brought The *War Cry* home regularly from the pub! Nobody else read it, only me!

My immersion in reading caused a sigh of relief. A neighbour feeling sorry for me in not having any *real books* gave me an old-fashioned thick Gothic Victorian romantic horror book with marvellous woodcut pictures. I read it three times, but I can't recall the title at present!

In a large family such as ours it was a case of sink or swim. Being a survivor, I set out to *swim and conquer*!

My gratitude to the Lord God Almighty is immense. I am for ever grateful that He chose to endow me with the wonder of normal hearing for *ten* years of my life – the years in which my language assimilation and comprehension and speech were formed. The *born deaf* are seriously deprived of these joys, which most persons take for granted. The average born deaf and childhood deaf are terribly disadvantaged even though they are 'normal'. The born deaf are wonderful people, cruelly deprived of what sets *Homo sapiens* above animals – the capacity of verbal communication. They are ordinary thinking human beings inside *glass bottles*. They can see and be seen, but sound passes them by. Without the joy of sound they have to learn to look for other compensations. It is to the great credit of the born deaf and early deafened – in fact, to all deaf people under the blanket term of *deaf* – that they climb the highest and hardest *mountains of life*, becoming good, clever people in their own right. They surmount obstacles and barriers of *invisible* things which an average person takes for granted. They, like me, use their eyes from the minute they wake up until lights-out at night. After lights-out we are *blind and deaf*! Every night of their lives, and mine too! People look at some of us elderly deaf and think our journey has been *easy* because we have conquered it! Pray do not be deluded. It has, and is, a lifetime of learning to cope and achieve the *impossible*! In overseas countries, especially in the developing world, life is very harsh for deaf people due to *survival of the fittest,* ignorance and fear of the unknown, just to mention a few reasons. And there is a lack of technology to aid them to a better life.

The world only has so many *tears to spare*, and those tears are usually reserved for whatever can be *seen and understood*. Sadly, deafness is still the Cinderella of disabilities. I suspect it always will be, due to its apparent invisibility.

But the deaf like me, who have the glory of speech and all which goes to make up life as it is generally known, must speak up on behalf of those who cannot *literally voice* their hopes and fears and needs. The old saying '*It takes one to know one*' could well apply to deafness! It takes another deaf person to know and understand exactly what being deaf means in its entirety.

I can remember my elderly (nearly ninety) mother-in-law once saying something about widowed women: "Only them that's lost know what it's like."

In like vein, only those who have lost their joy of hearing know what it's *actually like* to be deaf.

To make it clearer to hearing people, upon looking at someone with one leg it's no use you saying you know what it must be like, because you don't – you still have two legs!

There endeth the lesson!

Sunday mornings at *48* were joyous times. The radiogram or wireless (radio) emitted music and each member of the family sang. Only Peggy, the much loved family dog, never sang; but if dogs can smile, our Peggy smiled then!

Mother doled out the *day's orders*: "Eileen, peel those spuds; Queenie, shell those peas; Vilie [Violet], get stuck into some of that ironing. Those things need *doing*." And so it would go each and every Sunday morning. I would here add that as a *house rule* we girls ironed our own clothes. The clean washing was folded neatly and carefully piled high in the *usually locked* front room.

The *best room* was only used on special occasions or when the doctor was summoned! We didn't have many clothes – rationing was still on; you needed coupons!

Mother knitted her own woollens and helped us with ours. We had a warm coat and a coat for *work* if we were lucky. The best dress was washed and worn so often the boyfriends must have thought the girls only had one dress to their name! My sisters always looked a picture of elegance and good taste. Unless we were well groomed we didn't get past Mother's gimlet eye, let alone the front gate! My sisters swopped clothes regularly.

The two flat irons alternated on the gas cooker in summer or the fire in winter and gave off a simply gorgeous pungent aroma on the material being ironed, flashed swiftly and expertly over the cloth. I can smell it today. You had to test the iron by spitting on it. If the spittle sizzled and rolled off then the iron was hot enough! If it spat straight back at you – and it could! – then the iron was *too hot*!

Mother in the kitchen whipping up the Yorkshire-pudding batter would give a little twirl and a half-dance when singing along to the radiogram.

Father would be absorbed in his *silent* mutterings, reading the paper *aloud* to himself. We had all the Sunday newspapers – they were quite cheap then. Father was not in favour of us girls reading them. We had to wait until he was out of the way!

One Sunday for some reason or other to do with Fleet Street, I presumed, Mary came back without the Sunday papers. Dad being a bully (well, he had no sons!), with a filthy temper to boot, followed Mother into the garden. She was minding her own business just hanging a few oddments on the line to dry. Having nobody to blame about *his* Sunday papers, Dad took it out on his wife, our Mother! He had a filthy mouth and he used it. My sisters were aghast. He stopped Mother from re-entering the house and effed and blinded for all the world to hear, blaming Mother! The neighbours were hanging out of the back windows filled with horror! Talk about showing someone up. Father, you will by now have gathered, was an expert at that!

Then suddenly his face would smile and he'd pinch Mother's cheek *playfully* and tell her what a lovely old girl she was! He'd break into an old Cockney ditty, tell the *girls* to make a cup of tea, look up at the neighbours at their upstairs windows, smile affably and wave his hand, all friendly!

On other Sundays when reading the papers he would call out, "Turn that wireless-gram down. Listen to this, Em. Turn it DOWN! 'Ow d'yer expects yer muvver to 'ear wot I'm sayin'?"

He was an enigma of a man! I didn't hate him – I've never hated anyone in my life – but I had no feelings for him as a father! My father was Bill in Wales!

I was warned not to speak if he was telling Mother an anecdote from the day's paper. Unfortunately, he had a nasty habit of speaking loudly over anyone who was having an innocent conversation. Unfortunately, being deaf, I was apt not to stop as he talked louder and louder unbeknown to me, and before Mother or my sisters could warn me I was in hot water with a vengeance!

On Saturday mornings, if we got the chores done quickly and were lucky, us younger ones went to Saturday-morning pictures. I think it was only a few pence in old money – quite cheap for a few hours' entertainment. We went to the Odeon, and the queue of children stretched round the cinema in double lines. There was a film, cartoons and 'The Odeon Song'. Before the film started a white screen appeared with words of a ditty on it. A *ball* of light played on the words and we shouted and sang in unison with the words which the ball landed on.

The Odeon Song

From far and near we've gathered here
For the picture show.
What delight, all merry and bright,
But what we want to knoooow
Is everybody happy? YEEESSS!
Do we ever worry? NOOOOO!
To the Odeon we have come,
Now we're all together we can have some fun.
Do we help our neighbours? YEEESSS!
Do we ask for favours? NOOOOO!
We're a hundred thousand strong,
So how can we all be wrong?
We're members of the OCC [Odeon Cinema Club], we stress –
Is everybody happy? YEEESSSSSS!"

(I remember it from before I went deaf.)

The crescendo of the rousing last words almost raised the roof of the cinema! All children!

116

Out in the streets we played happily from morning to night on non-schooldays and weekends and after teatime was over. Hi, Jimmy Knacker, one, two, three was one game. Maybe that's why I have a bad back today! One person, legs astraddle, would lean against the front garden's three-foot-high wall, like being *frisked by the police*. Then all the children would jump on back after back, starting with the wall hugger, yelling out, "All over, all over." Imagine toads all on top of one female toad – at least ten of us piled on in that fashion. They were *innocent days* then (boys and girls together).

We played the game Queenie. One person stood out in front with his or her back to the rest. He or she would toss a ball backwards overhead, not knowing who caught the ball. We would all hold our hands behind our backs and yell, "Queenie!" The front person had to guess who had the ball. It was marvellous fun!

We played statues. One person took the outstretched arm and hand of each child and twisted and threw that person, whichever way the child fell, whether straight or doubled or whatever, the pose had to be held. The thrower would then go round trying to make you smile or laugh. If you did you were out.

Whip and top was a great favourite. If you hadn't a top you could improvise beautifully with a Tizer bottle top. Tizer was a popular children's and adults' drink. Tizer the appetiser, we called it. Whips were cheap to buy or make. Take a short length of stick, make a small hole at one end with a hot nail and thread a cord through – hey presto, a whip! The tops we coloured with coloured chalks cadged or *borrowed* from school! They made a pretty picture whirling around. We became wonderfully adept at keeping our tops in spinning motion. It was a neat trick to flip the whip a certain way, and the flick just tipped the side of the top and it spun and spun and spun. Whoever kept their top in motion the longest won the game. We played whips and tops for hours. It was a comparatively *quiet game*, apart from a few hollers of excitement; our mothers encouraged whip and top!

The pavements and roads were our playing grounds. Being traffic-free, more or less, and near our homes, it was an ideal situation. Today it would be impossible! Last time I visited *48* in 1994 the cars were bumper-to-bumper – with no gaps! – all down both sides of the road, hugging the pavements. It was the Christmas holidays and the men were not at work.

Marbles and cigarette cards or bus tickets were another childish amusement. We rolled the marbles along the gutters, avoiding (hopefully) the drains. (Many lost marbles down them!) We took turns to bend our thumb under our forefinger, flicking our thumbnail against the back of the forefinger's nail – from the knuckle, as it were. Getting down to the knuckle, as the saying goes. Away would roll your marble and hopefully and expectedly hit (or miss) your rival's marble in the gutter and you'd win that marble.

Cigarette-card flicking was a grand sport. Packets of cigarettes had special cards with film stars, sports stars, facts and other things on them, and you collected certain sets and swopped or bribed until you had a full set. You stood them slanted against a wall, then you placed a cigarette card in between your finger and forefinger and flicked it at the standing cards, knocking them down if you were expert at it.

There was a bus depot near the Fiddlers where we would pick up plenty of the old-fashioned flimsy card bus tickets in various colours. The colour of your bus ticket depended on how far you were travelling. The bus inspectors could tell at a glance if you had gone past your *legally paid* bus stop. Bus fares were cheap and buses were very frequent. Private cars were few and far between in our neck of the woods.

It was a simple matter to fold and twist the bus tickets until you ended up with a miniature concertina. The trick was to see how *long* you could make yours before it fell apart.

We went swimming over at Barking Lido. We didn't have access to pretty swimming costumes, but being good at improvisation we either stitched one or knitted one. I made a beautiful white woollen two-piece costume with a snazzy blue sailing boat Fair Isled in one corner. I was really proud of that costume. I'd spotted it in a woman's magazine, a weekly favourite magazine, and it is still going strong – not the costume, the magazine!

I lowered my posterior gently into the water, quite rightly proud of my beautiful costume. Even Mother had complimented me on my skill with my knitting needles. The wetter I got the more my pure woollen bikini-style bottom part of my costume dragged! It sagged and sagged and sagged.

In great embarrassment I climbed out of the pool beetroot-faced and my droopy drawers full of water were nearly down to my ankles from the weight! I was not the only one – there were others in the same boat! Whether it was due to the old unravelled re-knitted wool which I used, or whether it was meant to be just a *dry sunsuit*, I don't know, but I learnt my lesson about swimming costumes!

CHAPTER ELEVEN

At the end of January 1947 I entered a newer world within a deaf school community. I became a pupil at Tunmarsh Lane School for the Deaf, in Plaistow, E13, London. It eventually became, many, many years afterwards, the Newham School for the Deaf. It is now no more. I have been told it is used by social services. I was still not permitted (by my family) to go anywhere alone *due solely to my deafness*. I went to school on the school minibus. It picked me up at the door of *48* and it brought me back to *48* in the early evening after depositing other deaf children back at their own front doors. We had a lady attendant who was with us all the time. We were not allowed out of the minibus alone; the lady had to go to our front door with us and make sure our family were there. That was the law for deaf children and disabled children!

Our school's official name was West Ham School for the Deaf, but we always called it Tunmarsh Lane School because it was in Tunmarsh Lane near the Greengate. We always knew when we were nearing Tunmarsh Lane before our minibus turned into it. The smell of the sweet factory at the entrance of the lane made our mouths water.

It was now for me a transition from the world of the hearing to the world of the deaf. *It was an amazingly happy transition.* The school was more of a family of perhaps no more than about thirty-five children, I do not recall the exact number. I would mention the NHS hearing aid was not available to the best of my memory and knowledge. (No NHS in 1947.) You will thus understand when I tell you later on how they *tested* our hearing range. The headmistress was a tiny shrivelled-up old lady called Miss Mullen. Her age was indeterminate to us. She was kind but strict.

I found myself in a classroom of deaf children of various ages! I was eleven years old.

They are still alive, so if I have mistaken their ages in 1947 I apologise. Deaf children stayed at schools for the deaf one extra year by law – meaning sixteen if others left at fifteen and seventeen if others left at sixteen. That is how it went. The normal hearing children's school leaving age was soon to be fifteen years.

Miss Brink was my teacher – a real lavender-and-lace (kind of) dedicated professional teacher. Her father had been Dutch and she had a deaf sister. They lived in 10 Acland Road, Willesden Green, London. All my *deaf life* up to her death in old age, long after I had moved to Norfolk, Miss Brink was the first person after my Welsh family to send me a Christmas card. She was a lovely lady, firm yet fair. She wore a floral cotton long-sleeved overall to keep the chalk off her clothes. Indeed I never met any other student from West Ham School for the Deaf who didn't like Miss Brink. She never appeared fazed or shouted or was nasty. She *would not tolerate unseemly behaviour just because a child was deaf*. We were treated as what we were: *human beings with closed-off ears*. She was not against smacking lightly the hand of an extra-nasty or unruly child – they were never nasty or unruly again, because they really did love and respect her. Miss Brink was of the old school of very competent teachers which today are either a dying breed or, in some places, as dead as the fabled dodo. Miss Brink was lovely!

Another teacher loved and respected was Mr Lee. He invented a *sound system* to use in his classroom. Deaf people usually have difficulty in knowing how loudly or softly they are speaking, especially before NHS hearing aids became available. He used the system on his classes long after I left the school in 1949. Proof was when we went back for a reunion one of his old pupils, now a working lad in the wide world, was speaking too loudly – Mr Lee merely spoke softly to him using one word, a certain colour, and the boy nodded, thanked Mr Lee and spoke more quietly. We all loved Mr Lee. Indeed I cannot recall any of our teachers whom we did not love. The whole ambience of our school was loving and caring, combined with education to help children cope to the best of their individual abilities depending on their range of deafness and speech.

I have been told by the secretary that I started there on 27 January 1947. I found it a blessing that my introduction to deaf *society* was at our school in Plaistow; I have for ever been grateful to the teachers and other staff. (The secretary was called Mrs Hutchinson.)

There is great illiteracy amongst deaf children – more so in 1947. Hopefully with the introduction of having deaf children in a unit attached to a mainstream school this may one day be overcome. I was recently told that the reading and writing capability of *average deaf* children is still that of an eight-year-old when they are sixteen years old. I hope it is not true. I know we have to fit into a hearing world when we leave school, so going to the new units will make it easier. I don't really know. But I am *glad I went to a school for the deaf* because it enabled me to have the love and friendship and understanding of my disability without causing me hurt and embarrassment. My long years of life have taught me how difficult it is to cope in the hearing world. I have good speech; what must it be like for those with poor education and poor speech? One always has to be extra-alert, smile when the joke is at one's expense (on account of deafness) and work harder at everything, even if it's only going shopping in the hearing world! One's eyes are constantly *on parade* – they have to duplicate for our ears. Tension and frustration are double when you are deaf. If the deaf with poor speech cannot get to mingle with their *own* kind at clubs or school then they do not get a proper chance of relaxation. Maybe that is what some of the older deaf mean when they say the closure of schools for the deaf is wrong. *I* truly don't know the answer; but then, I have good speech and ten years of normal hearing life to back me up. Who am I to dispute with those older deaf people? May I state that I am totally grateful for both of the schools for the deaf which I was so fortunate to attend? Without what they did for me my life might have turned out bleak rather than fulfilled, as it has been.

Because I was a good reader, Miss Brink would make up stories with her own excellent and charming illustrations in exercise books. She did everything she could to foster my love of the written word. We never attended public libraries from school and Father would not let me go to the one near *48* because he didn't want to *pay any fines*!

When I was much older I did go in one once, not far from *48*. It was an awe-inspiring world with a big notice saying, '*SILENCE PLEASE*'. The room smelt of polish. I felt I was in another world altogether. The lady behind the counter looked at me over the top of her glasses and asked me a question. I pointed to my ears and she cottoned on. Then she wrote on a piece of paper, 'Do you wish to become a member of this library?' I nodded then shook my head. She was mystified and her eyebrows rose questioningly.

Like a conspirator, I looked furtively around the room. Nobody was watching me. I said, "I'm deaf. Deaf people can't join libraries, can they?"

She smiled and wrote, "Why not?"

A lump stuck in my throat. "Because Father said I'd have to pay fines and I don't know what fines are." They sounded like something ominous to me!

She tried not to smile again and wrote down, "Fines are small sums of money if you are late returning your books. Would you like a membership card?"

I didn't know what a membership card was either, but I felt sure Father wouldn't like that any more than the *horror* of fines. She showed me one and said my parents had to sign it. Knowing Father wouldn't sign or allow Mother to I reluctantly shook my head, gave her a sweet smile and crept from *the hallowed hall*.

Nevertheless I felt good! At last I had been brave enough to venture into a library and had been accepted as a normal human being. It must have subconsciously had a profound effect on my psyche. In the seventies and part of the sixties I worked as a librarian assistant for thirteen and a half years (1967–80)!

Whenever I see or read the poem 'A Boy's Song' by James Hogg I recall dear Miss Mabel Brink. It was she who introduced me to it as one of her favourites. Who can forget the descriptive first lines:

'Where the pools are bright and deep,
Where the grey trout lies asleep . . .'

When I went into teaching adults in later life, this was one of the favourite poems which I *slung* at my *advanced classes*, and it was a popular choice – almost as popular as the seasonal one I *slung* at them:

''Twas the night before Christmas, when all through the house,
Not a creature was stirring, not even a mouse!'

What beautiful thoughts I am privileged to have in my store of memories of yesteryears. Miss Brink did me a great service by giving me *homework* (the others didn't get the same!) and *encouraging me to use my speech* and retain it intact. We were of mixed ages in our class. She was very fond of Mabel Lucie Attwell's drawings and gave me some – I don't know where they went to along life's way. It gave me a love of them.

At my first deaf school I met many kinds of deaf children. We had a little chap who had one blue eye and one brown eye. It was like looking at two different people according to which side of him you sat! To this day if anyone says, *"One blue eye, one brown eye,"* we know who is meant.

Deaf people give *sign names* to one another and whomsoever they are referring to. If a person had a very dimpled chin like Kirk Douglas then they would point to their chin so we knew whom they were referring to. Today because of my married name they point to their foot when talking about me. Princess Diana had hair brushed back by her ears so they sign the brushed-back sign and they still say, "Lady Diana". I guess that is easier to speak than "Princess".

I was not too long at the school when Miss Mullen retired and Miss V. Kathleen Mitchell became our new headmistress – a new broom.

Miss Mullen had the weird idea that it was good for us to stamp as we walked out of the hall after morning assembly! We were in drill lines of house colours: blue, green, yellow and red. I was captain of the yellow house. Miss Mullen, a tiny wizened lady, started the usual stamping process herself by saying loudly, and moving in time to her beating hand (like a musical conductor), "One, two, three, FOUR!" We picked our feet up, bent our knees and started on our left foot in military style! On the count of four we banged our right leg and foot down on the ground as hard as we could! And so we marched from the assembly hall with little Miss Mullen stamping alongside each consecutive drill line. If we didn't stamp hard enough we had to go back into lines and start all over again!

Maybe she felt the vibrations from the polished wooden flooring were beneficial to us as a form of *sound vibrations?* At assembly we held our hands together for prayers, but were permitted to keep our eyes open so we could lip-read.

To instil music and rhythm in us we had a glorious vivacious teacher who taught us with tambourines, for vibrations. We may not have been perfect, but I can assure you of our happiness and enthusiasm for the country folk dancing. It was one of the highlights of our week. 'Rufty Tufty' was one of the teacher's favourites. It brings a smile to certain faces today if we mention folk dancing. I don't think we were any threat to any of the traditional Morris dancers. I certainly recommend country dancing for a happy form of exercise.

In our classroom there were a few large white butler sinks (nowadays people call them Belfast sinks). The room was used by the cookery teacher to teach the older girls the merits and rewards of cooking good wholesome meals, how to lay the table and wash the crockery and utensils. Each week a different group cooked dinner for themselves and the teacher. This, needless to say, was a popular class! About six pupils cooked dinner each week. There were two cookers to make it easier in teaching. Two girls could prepare the vegetables and keep an eye on them cooking; two girls prepared the meat, which to my memory nearly always consisted of meat rissoles when it was my turn! Mincemeat mixed with a beaten egg was rolled in breadcrumbs after chopped onions had been added with a few herbs and spices, salt and pepper; the mixture was shaped like sausages and fried in a frying pan with best fresh beef dripping purchased from the butcher. Today on a television cooking programme that method would be beautifully, succinctly described as *pan-fried*!

Earlier, after assembly, the *chosen* went to the local shops at the bottom of Tunmarsh Lane, beside the main road, where we were initiated into the *housewifely art* of purchasing the ingredients for our meal, which we were going to cook ourselves. Nobody we knew had fridges or freezers in their own homes. It was standard procedure for women to purchase *daily* their shopping requirements, with fresh meat from the butcher.

In those days *deaf children and other disabled children were very sheltered from the ordinary realities of life!*

Our teacher showed us how to lay the table, with the knives and forks and spoons in their correct places, and to place a linen table napkin in the correct position at each place setting. To this very day, even when dining alone, I never have a meal without a table napkin!

A very important procedure dealt with the table knives. They were not *all-in-one steel knives* which are widely used in modern times; they had ivory handles, and were precious to the teacher. I think they were real ivory, but they could have been something resembling it. The teacher *always* made us fill a straight-sided jug with hot soapy water. When we had finished the first course one of us had to collect the knives and place them in the jug so the *cutting* metal parts of the knives were immersed in the water and the handles stood proudly free. During washing-up time the handles would be individually wiped with a warm dishcloth.

In a full-length walk-in cupboard in our classroom, Miss Brink kept all the sewing materials and a beautiful china doll. That doll was used by Miss Brink to teach us how to wash and change a baby, and to make clothes for it. I made many outfits for that doll. To handle the doll was a form of *bribery reward* for doing well at speaking and lip-reading.

Miss Brink was a very, very versatile teacher, teaching us reading, writing, geography, sewing and embroidery. She instilled a love of the art of crewel embroidery in me; to wit I have many crewel-embroidered pictures on my walls which I made in adult life. Over the years I also embroidered numerous chair-back covers, but I have not got one to my name! I gave them all away to people who asked for them! I love the art of *giving* and felt *sorry* for *visitors* who said *they* couldn't sew. With hindsight I realise I should have encouraged them to learn to sew and embroider. I did try sometimes, but they always seemed to have an excuse, like *not having the time*, which on honest reflection seems to be the standard excuse for many of our population! Miss Mullen's retirement was due, and Miss Brink set me to work hand-stitching and braiding a felt tea cosy as a present from Miss Brink's class.

Her replacement was a wonderful teacher and headmistress, Miss V. Kathleen Mitchell from Brighouse in Yorkshire, whom I and many of her other students kept in touch with via cards and photos until she died in January 1998 aged ninety-one at her deceased father's house in Brighouse. Some students, including Rosalia Robb (née Baker), managed to drive and see her before she passed over to the other side. I understand that she could remember all of us and only one of our crowd had she ever lost touch with. That was my old school friend Evelyn Weston. Nobody knows what happened to Evelyn. We were Miss Mitchell's school *family*. It is quite a lovely touch that most deaf children educated at schools for the deaf have managed to keep in contact with their teachers and old school friends. And *that* is one of the forms of *camaraderie* which many older deaf people are fearful will be lost with Partially Hearing Units (PHU) instead of schools for the deaf. On the other hand, *integration into* the real world is of paramount importance; but whether the PHUs are *the answer*, bearing in mind the solitude imposed by deafness and the need for deaf people to be able to relax with their own kind, is a bit of a conundrum. *I* do not have the answer to it!

Miss Mitchell was almost always smiling, a plumpish, short, energetic soul who would bend over backwards to help *her children* – us! She was in a similar mould to Miss Brink and Mr Lee and the other teachers, whose names at present escape me. They were teachers who knew how to control their charges, and how to actually teach, which teachers are paid to do – to teach and instil knowledge into children's heads. Of course, possibly due to their deafness and poor speech, there were some children who did not learn much academically, but they did learn to cope with their handicaps and were treated and accepted as human beings in a far-off age when it was still considered *normal* to put a deaf person into an institution for life!

Our teachers and all *deaf teachers*, as we lovingly termed them, believed strongly that the deaf were and are educable; we owe much to their strong belief and pioneering examples. Us!

As we have grown over the years, and had and *raised* families and grandchildren of our own, we are the wonderful *living yardstick* of their belief in our being educable human beings. Enlightened peoples now, through us, do not, I hope, consider us as the deaf and dumb, to be put into asylums for ever. In living memory that has been known to be done!

Miss Mitchell had *further-education* plans for some of her deaf students, this being *a further advancement of the deaf*, proving their capacity for higher and university education. The pioneer teachers of the deaf were to be proved correct: deafness as a disability *does not necessarily* preclude deaf children from the highest echelons of education ability and opportunities.

Miss Mitchell and Miss Brink told me they wanted me to take an entrance examination for the Mary Hare Grammar School for the Deaf, which was going to move to larger premises and expand with more students from its school in Burgess Hill, Sussex, to Arlington Manor near Newbury in Berkshire. This was to be, and still is, the National Grammar School for the Deaf, now called the Mary Hare School. It is a unique school, founded in 1946 on the death of Miss Mary Hare and her Oral School for Deaf Children at Burgess Hill, Sussex.

Miss Hare was called *Birdie* by her friends because of her thick hair, and by all accounts she was a handsome and enlightened woman. Her great friend, and another teacher, was Miss Smart. In Brighton Miss Hare was the president of the local branch of theosophy and was a theosophist. Her Oral School for Deaf

Children, a private school at Dene Hollow, was famous for its enlightened education of deaf children. There were some thirty students at Dene Hollow at any one time.

A child of three had been brought all the way from South Africa to be taught orally, and when Miss Hare told her to *demonstrate* to people how she could *talk* the child said, "How do you do?" quite clearly.

In the days when the deaf and mentally deranged were often confused Miss Hare had been instrumental in *saving* many good deaf children from a *life of the mentally insane.* She proved conclusively, by her pioneering work and strong belief, that the deaf are educable. She opened up the world for deaf education. She has been proved correct countless times over the ensuing years and we, the deaf, have benefited from the remarkable grammar school which she bestowed upon the nation (her 'Oral School'), to be henceforth known as the Mary Hare Grammar School for the Deaf. In later years the word 'deaf' was legally allowed to be left off the school sign – another triumph for the deaf and their tutors.

Miss Mitchell and Miss Brink discovered that the school was to take in more students in its new larger premises, and was taking in those over the age of eleven, which today is the usual age for most boarding-school entrance examinations. They had decided that I was intelligent and clever enough to merit sitting the entrance examination. I am for ever grateful to Miss Brink and Miss Mitchell and my mother, who *forged* Father's signature!

He had said, "The uvvers ain't been to grammar school so why should you? Anyway youse is a girl and education don't matter for a girl. Don't go getting ideas above yer station!"

Therefore I became the *first* pupil of West Ham School for the Deaf to take the entrance examination to the Mary Hare Grammar School for the Deaf. Somebody had to be first – I was just lucky.

Miss Mitchell smilingly took me into an empty classroom and sat me down with the examination questions and lots of pencils, pens, ink and rulers and rubbers. I took the written examination of the Mary Hare Grammar School.

Unbeknown to Father, I passed the written examination. It was subtly arranged that instead of my parents accompanying me for the oral examination, my dear teacher Miss Brink was to have the honour. On the train to Sussex I think Miss Brink, bless her, was as excited as I was, because she was going to actually *see* the Oral School for the Deaf! I was amazed to be accompanied round the school by a well-mannered nicely dressed girl wearing a green gingham dress with a white collar and a green cardigan. I had met my first (Jeanne Romeril) *higher-educated* deaf person! Wow! I was bowled over. She actually spoke very well from a lip-reading point of view – I do not know about her voice. None of the children used sign language, and yet they communicated! Even more wow!

My conducted tour brought us to a room of other children, all chatting without sign language! I was oral because I had already acquired speech by the age of ten and my teachers encouraged my speech at all times. Indeed, Father would hit my hands with his slipper (it hurt) if I attempted any of the signs which I had naturally picked up from other deaf children! *Deaf children will always sign amongst themselves*!

But children at this oral school were another kettle of fish. My lip-reading skill still left much to be desired. I watched in amazed astonishment and almost disbelief at children (and some were sixteen years old) speaking *fluently* amongst themselves from mouth to mouth – and no sign language! I thought they were the bee's knees. I fervently hoped against hope that I would pass my oral examination that day and that Father would consent to my joining that obviously elite band of deaf persons.

Not understanding one of the students in the course of general chit-chat, my escort waved her hand and wrote on the blackboard, 'Don't worry, we will write down for you because you are not as skilled as us!' I thought that was kind of her, and made no demur when she pulled up four chairs and motioned me to sit on one and put my feet up on another. "Rest," she said. "Don't worry – everything will be all right." She must have been a mind reader!

My turn for the oral examination soon came and I entered a room full of distinguished-looking oral teachers of the deaf. They were quite friendly and asked me many seemingly innocuous questions, making written notes all the while. In front of the principal, Mr Mundin, there were two ornaments: a statue of the Venus de Milo and a pottery grinning frog.

"Which of these do you prefer and like, Violet?"

My eyes lighted on Venus and dismissed her quickly; reasoning that I did not know who or what she represented, and as I had never seen it before, I played safe and replied, "The frog, sir."

"And why is that, Violet?" from another teacher, who spoke slowly and carefully.

"Because the frog is smiling and looking happy and cheerful, sir!"

"Hm! You like cheerful, happy things, Violet?"

"Yes, sir!"

Finally my oral examination was at an end. I thanked the principal, Mr Mundin, who said, "We shall look forward to seeing you again soon, Violet!"

I nodded my head, grateful to depart before I put my foot in it, *not realising* he had more or less told me *in advance* that I had been accepted!

Miss Brink, who'd been conducted over the school by another teacher and some of the pupils, could barely conceal her excitement as we sat in the railway carriage being *chuffed* back to London. She questioned me lengthily and smiled and said, "Well done, Violet. Miss Mitchell will be overjoyed. I am so happy for you, my dear!"

I thought we were being a *trifle premature* in that I still had to wait for the official confirmation in writing!

Miss Brink told me an outline about Miss Mary Hare and of her sister Ethel Hare, who was also a pioneer in oralism for the deaf. She had helped her sister for many years. Ethel, a teacher, had taught hard-of-hearing children at several schools for the hard of hearing and she worked at the Hugh Myddelton School in London. When the Second World War broke out Ethel had already retired. Then she went to Dene Hollow to help her sister Mary Hare.

Some years later, when I was a pupil at Arlington Manor (the new premises of the school), I recall a load of books being delivered in huge trunks as being *left to the school by the late Miss Ethel Hare.*

Jean Goadsby, who became Jean Sellers (Jean sadly died several years ago, about 2013), lived in Lincolnshire and came to see me from time to time. She was a pupil of Miss Hare's from the age of three years at Dene Hollow. Jean had a fantastic memory – well, she did go to boarding school from three to eighteen years! *Fifteen years* of the cream of teachers educated her! Jean remembered Miss Hare's lovely green eyes and her beautiful smile, and she said they knew her favourite colour was green – hence the school's tradition of green for the school uniform of the girls and the badge and ties of the boys and girls at Arlington. Jean told me they always called Miss Hare by her Christian name, Mary. Jean was the last child to say *goodbye* to Mary and kiss her cold freckled hand. In the morning Annie, Mary's faithful deaf servant, who worshipped

Mary, woke Jean up and told her that Mary was dead. Jean, like the other children, burst into tears and they went into the sitting room, which was full of wreaths and flowers, but she did not see the coffin. Jean had been taught by Mary for five years. Jean said the ashes of Mary's body are in St John's Church.

Without Mary Hare it is quite possible that we higher-educated deaf may never have had the opportunity to have a thorough education, as we undoubtedly have had and still do.

Meanwhile I waited anxiously for the actual *acceptance* letter. I wondered what Father would do and could hardly contain myself for the excitement my future now held for me!

CHAPTER TWELVE

Now it was to be *Per oculos non aures* for me at my wondrous new school. (Through eyes not ears.)

My lip-reading was still poor compared to the standard of lip-reading I encountered at the Mary Hare Grammar School. I am today judged to be an *expert* lip-reader. I don't think one can be entirely *expert* in lip-reading because it depends on whom you are *reading*, how far you are from that person or persons, how fresh or tired you feel, if you are reading at night or in the daytime, if the person is sitting or standing in a favourable position *without* their back to the light, and many other factors.

Being a tolerant person and not plagued by a plethora of likes and dislikes in my daily life, I do admit I hate lip-reading somebody who is wearing dark glasses, because I cannot read their darned face properly and I find it unnerving to have to gaze at somebody's dark sunglasses when having a conversation. It seems bad manners to my mind if a person does not *need* to wear dark glasses but deliberately wears them when talking to a deaf person! It makes lip-reading much harder, because only about a third of words fully show on the lips; the rest is face-reading, and the eyes, as part of the face, are eloquent *in silence*.

In my last school report I have C- beside the words 'lip-reading skill'! It is therefore feasible and truthful to state that lip-reading did not come easily and joyfully to me: I had to work at it!

May I say that any deaf or hard-of-hearing person reading this *may take hope* if their own skill at lip-reading is not yet too great!

I think having to learn French via lip-reading is enough to try the patience of a saint! Then there are the works of Shakespeare and all those long speeches to be lip-read! I took *Macbeth* at O level and the lip-reading of the important speeches has stayed with me today, and will for ever! I was never any good at French, I may add!

October 1949 arrived soon enough. I was to become a pupil of the Mary Hare Grammar School at long last. I had lived in England and Wales, in London and Essex, and now I was going to live in Berkshire. Wow! Mother had bought me a stout pair of brown brogues with the new fashionable innovation of thick crêpe soles from Barratt's shoe shop. Father being out of work, the council had instructed my mother that I would be provided with all my clothes *when I reached the school*! The council had granted me a clothing grant and the long list of clothing and sports things required, which Mother had a list of, *would be all taken care of.* Mother took this *literally* to mean that all would be awaiting my arrival!

This was not to be! Father had *conveniently lost* (I didn't believe him – would you?) the money which the council had provided to pay our railway fares to Newbury.

I bowled up the long, stately, curving shingled driveway of Arlington Manor sitting in the back of a greengrocery van with the tarpaulin sides rolled up, to be confronted by a car dealer's dream of swanky cars drawn up outside the Manor House! Perhaps we should have gone round to the tradesmen's entrance in the open-backed van! We were sitting on empty orange crates! I don't remember it bothering me unduly because everything was so new and strange. The route we had taken had been through some lovely parts of England long gone under the concrete of modern motorways. Looking back, I feel privileged to have witnessed England as it was then!

I did feel a bit awkward when it came to clothing. All I had was what I stood up in: the red jumper or blouse and black gymslip of West Ham School for the Deaf (uniform)! I did have my smashing new slip-on brogues, a new pair of clean white socks, a flannel and soap, but nothing else that I can recall!

Mother had the grace to say that if she had known she would have cadged some of my sisters' clothes off them for me!

So I wore my *same clothes* for quite some time, and it was embarrassing at weekends because in the evenings on Saturdays we were permitted to wear our own clothes, provided it was a blouse or jumper and skirt and we wore a compulsory dress on Sundays! We had lots of social weekend activities. I was able to stick out like a sore thumb when every girl was in *mufti* and I wore an old school uniform! They also wore stockings in the week – thick brown lisle ones – with the green gymslips in winter. As the only girl in a black gymslip and no stockings it was a bit upsetting!

The measurement for uniforms – and this included thick green interlock knickers – was done by a man from a large store in London! We had to hold our gymslips up whilst he measured us for our knickers and *corsets* and bras! I don't know who was the more embarrassed, us or him?

Finally I was kitted with three pairs of pink cotton pyjamas and three pairs of dark-green interlock knickers with the customary pocket on the right leg in which we had to keep our daily handkerchief! There were no tissues! I also had one pair of corsets and three pairs of bras of an indeterminate shade of flesh colour, literally looking like a *hammock for two*. The uplift bra only came after Jane Russell, the film star, wore uplift bras in the film *The Outlaws*, which caused some cries of outrage when the posters of her cleavage and open necked blouse were shown on the billboards! Hers had been invented by that filthy-rich bloke who became an eccentric *fear-of-germs* recluse – Howard Hughes.

Many women never wore bras until they were well into their forties; they just wore a vest!

Our introduction to uplift bras at school came via *Sheila*, of one of the lower forms! This was at a later age, not in 1949!

I had to have one good-quality dark-green Burberry raincoat, one dark-green woollen blazer, one matching tam-o'-shanter (beret), one long thick green-and-yellow-striped scarf in wool, one matching pair of dark-green gloves, three white Viyella blouses with long sleeves and a pocket on one side of the chest, three white cellular-cotton short-sleeved sports blouses, one pair of dark-green twill divided skirts (shorts), three warm interlock vests, a pair of white plimsolls and a pair of black plimsolls. The hockey stick and shoes and lacrosse sticks were part and parcel of our belongings, but I think the school supplied most of this sort of stuff. I did not have a tennis racquet of my own. The three green-checked gingham dresses with white Peter Pan collars and all the other clothes came from the council grant.

After I left school in 1953 the Civic Centre of Dagenham wrote me nice letter congratulating me on making the most of my abilities, which I thought was most decent of them seeing that *they* paid for my education and my clothing.

At weekends and parties the girls wore pretty dresses. Great was my excitement when my eldest sister, Emmie, made me a turquoise taffeta dress piped in red satin, and posted it all the way from America along with a wonderful real candlewick dressing gown in a greenish blue!

Nobody else got parcels from America, only me! At school, I mean. It was quite exciting when parcels or Emmie's letters arrived because there were avid stamp collectors amongst the boys and girls! I became *popular* each time some stamps came from the USA! I also had a letter with an inexpensive brooch in it – what Americans term *a pin*, a piece of costume jewellery. When the duty prefect collected the post and handed it out (before we got our *pigeonholes* under the main staircase, which is no longer there; a study is there now for Matron) there was some saucy banter as we all tried to guess what was in my bulky envelope.

I *absolutely adored* boarding school! I really did! I was one of the few girls who did not cry the first night back at the start of each new term! I don't remember Audrey crying either – she loved school too.

Today I look back, as do many others, with warmth and nostalgia for the excellent teachers we had. Some whose names I can easily recall are Mr Askew, Miss Hall, Miss Cragg, Mrs Askew, Mr Salt, Mr Bates, Mr Dolton, Mr Barratt, Mr Hill, Mr Brown, Mr Ainge, Mr Shirley and Miss Gardiner. There are some whose names escape me. Our men teachers had been captains and pilots in the war years.

In 1949 the war had only been over for four years. Our teachers were very into discipline, but they never laid a hand on us. In modern parlance (speak) they were *great*. Used to organising servicemen under their command, they organised and taught us as teachers should teach. They imparted knowledge. If we got caught up in a few wartime reminiscences, so what? We still learnt something, didn't we?

After Mary Hare's death, when a board of trustees was set up, in 1946, Sir Fred Clarke in his speech on speech day in the November said, "We are trying to liberate the innate intelligence which lies within so many deaf children. With this liberation we hope for increased opportunities for the individuals. And, also, that our old pupils may go forth and be like unto the leaven which a woman hid in three measures of meal: until the whole was leavened."

Well, if Sir Fred Clarke was here today as I write this updated autobiography of mine, I could tell him that at the fiftieth reunion of the 1946–56 old pupils at the Bedford Hotel in November 1986 (London) a couple of hundred of us turned up and all have made successes of our lives and have good marriages, wonderful grown-up children and grandchildren. Graham from Scotland has three sons by his deaf wife and two of the sons are medical GPs, which I think is fantastic.

I can almost imagine I can see Miss Mary Hare, Miss Ethel Hare, Mr Mundin and Mr Askew smiling down proudly from heaven saying, "We have been proved right: the deaf are intelligent."

We had a beautiful stately polished staircase in the entrance hall, which actually (the hall) was used for assemblies. That is not the case today. In my era we had the Manor House for our dormitories, our classrooms and our dining room and some single bedrooms for unmarried tutors.

By the kind permission of the present principal we had a summer reunion of old pupils from any era with a tree-planting ceremony and a splendid buffet and other things in 1996. I felt, like many of my generation, how sad it was to see the pretty common room with its dividing doors now part of a coffee bar! It was sad, and it upset many of us to witness some of the modern changes – especially the change of the school colours and uniform! It's sad to know the splendid *aristocratic*-looking school badge has been changed. We old ones still have great pride in our old school badges. The girls' bedrooms were another shock!

I suppose one has to move with the times, but it's so sad to change the school colours and the proud badge with the 'MHGS' on it; after all, the historical schools in London spring to my mind which today still wear the uniform worn since their historical foundation hundreds of years ago. Green was the favourite colour of our beloved founder, Miss Mary Hare. Without her there would have been no grammar school or higher education for the deaf in Britain! Some traditions should not be thrown out with the bath water if they are not harmful to anybody!

Other than that I would like to pay my respects and thanks to the teachers and staff and headmaster and pupils at the fiftieth reunion of the old pupils (1996) at Arlington. They made us feel so welcome we were loth to leave. It was a bit of a wrench to go! They and the OPA, who arranged the actual reunion, did us proud.

I have always loved Maeterlinck's Bluebird of Happiness, which has always been part of our school badge. It was said that Mary Hare *abounded in happiness*, like the Bluebird, because she was always radiant – a lovely woman. Mr F. L. Denmark, who was concerned in the founding of the school, gave an address and spoke

135

of his friendship and admiration for Mary Hare (1949) before the school left Sussex.

He said, "We have praised famous men. . . . Now I speak of a woman who will be famous wherever and whenever deaf children are educated, for Mary Hare was truly a great woman. She was an outstanding teacher, a wise counsellor, and a sincere friend, and her fine presence was in accord with her beautiful nature. She possessed dignity and deportment, two qualities which appear to be growing less and less in so many cases but which, I am glad to see, play no small part in the work of the school which bears her name. Her initials are woven *in the emblem* of the school, but *they* are more than initials. Mary is one of those beautiful old names which are fast disappearing and it is seldom now given to a girl. But in *her case, if M stands for Mary it also means Mother* for in very truth, Mary Hare mothered the children in her charge. And if H stands for Hare it also means *happiness*: for Mary Hare radiated abounding happiness both in her school and amongst her friends. Nevertheless . . . that while the spirit of Mary Hare remains as I am sure it will remain, all will be well; and the school shall serve as a permanent memorial to Mary Hare."

I rest my case for the retaining of the colour green and Miss Hare's initials on the school badge.

In 1949 I entered the fourth form at the Mary Hare Grammar School *for the Deaf*, as it was legally known. The common room was divided in the daytime by two folding doors, making it into two classrooms. After evening *prep* and supper the doors were opened and we had *fun*!

Some of the boys wrestled, and the girls did, well, whatever girls do! The girls' dormitories and bathrooms were in the main part of the Manor House and on the same floor, which also had Mr Mundin's (the principal) flat for himself and his wife. He was a very kindly man, but I was not to know him for long!

There were girls' dormitories up a short flight of stairs and the boys' dormitories down a short flight of stairs. The bedrooms thus were on three levels, which could be reached by either the *grand staircase* or the back staircase. We were normally only permitted to use the *grand staircase* on special occasions as you will read later. A door (unlocked) separated the boys' floor from the girls'.

Nowadays (in the nineties) except for the very youngest boys the bulk of the boys live in their own modern block, which has their bathrooms and their own dining room and kitchen.

In my time, 1949–53, we all lived, ate and slept in the Manor House like a small family – about sixty-five of us, boys and girls together. We only separated for bedrooms. Some of the dormitories were called Edgar Mundin, Thomas Arnold, Mary Hare, Ethel Hare, Helen Keller and Thomas Braidwood – all eminent people in the world of deafness and education.

The school was divided into four houses:

Mary Hare = green
Thomas Arnold = red
St John of Beverley = yellow.
Thomas Braidwood = blue.

I was in St John of Beverley, which was yellow.

During my first academic year at Mary Hare Grammar School, it was a terrible shock to us all when Mr Mundin died. Whenever it is daffodil time I think of Wales and Mr Mundin and my late dear husband, Fred. At Easter time 1950 Mr Mundin, wearing his old raincoat, arose early and went out to pick daffodils, which abounded at our school. We were in the hall waiting for the school bus to take us to the railway station at Newbury, about three miles distant. Mr Mundin tied the daffodils into bunches and gave each of us a bunch with his own hands, *for our mothers*. With his sweet smile he bade us goodbye and patted our cheeks (girls) and shook the boys' hands. We waved goodbye cheerily and went off home for the Easter holidays.

On a Sunday in the holidays Father had a shock! He couldn't believe his eyes! He read of the death of Mr Mundin in one of the national papers. Whether it was the *News of the World* or *Reynolds News* or one of the others (because he had them all) I cannot recollect. I would not believe it until he *permitted* me to read it for myself! I confess, I did cry. Poor Mr Mundin – such a lovely man! The story was that he had been climbing over a rickety little gate in the Dell opposite the Manor House front door and his shotgun exploded! His dog Tinker, a very plump happy black Labrador was whining, and that is how he was found dead!

He remains in my memory and that of many of us as we last saw him in his old shapeless fawn raincoat and his wellington boots, picking daffodils!

That was possibly the first death I ever knew of or related to in my life. It was hard to understand it.

There was a memorial fund and books, and bookplates with his photo on were pasted inside all of the books in his memory. I have one in my photo album.

We never did know what happened to his wife after Mr Mundin died so tragically.

Our senior teacher/tutor, Mr Raymond Askew, succeeded Mr Mundin after his untimely death. Raymond Askew was a tall, strict but fair and kindly man, a former captain in the armed forces. He *expected to be obeyed*, but you knew where you were with him. Like Mr Mundin and some of the other tutors he played cricket for the school and was in the football team. Mr Askew's main subject was science, but I am afraid it was not my best one! I still remember that acids turn blue litmus red and bases turn red litmus blue because he drummed it into me! During one of our experiments, with the Bunsen burner in the science laboratory we made an awful compound, which absolutely nauseatingly ponged to high heaven! Mr Askew told us to imagine it smelt like Californian Poppy Perfume, which was a popular perfume of our era!

When it came to writing up our notes at prep that evening I innocently wrote in that Mr Askew had alluded to the pong as smelling like *Californian Poppy Perfume*. He roared with laughter when he read my write-up the next time! He said to remember not to write *that* in my matriculation examinations! I could think of no way that I would ever get anywhere at science, let alone as part of matriculation, which meant you had to pass certain core subjects. If you failed one you failed the lot! The Lord God Almighty must have heard my prayers of supplication: matriculation was dropped for O levels with a pass mark of about 45! This meant that eventually I was allowed to drop science, maths and French and concentrate on my English language, English literature, art, social economic history (good, as I knew nothing about kings and queens!), which I love, and religious knowledge, which I failed by two marks. I got a pass mark of 70% in social economic history. English language, English literature and art I passed very well indeed, but I forget the marks.

We took the Oxford Local Examinations General Certificate of Education. I took mine in 1953. In the same year to my immense surprise I got the Form Prize VA.

In 1952 I was awarded the Social Services Prize. In 1952 the school had a demonstration of dancing and drama: an English country dance, a *fandango* by senior girls, then a scene from

Treasure Island (that was the black spot at the Admiral Benbow Inn), another English country dance ('The Morpeth Rant', by junior girls), then the sleepwalking scene from *Macbeth* and a Scottish country dance ('The Glasgow Highlanders' by senior girls).

Mrs Askew was a beautiful dancer (of Scottish reels), imparting her knowledge to deaf students of differing degrees of deafness. There were no post-aural hearing aids available at that time. Most students were totally deaf anyway. (We did have the bulky Medrescos.)

Mr Askew, our principal, had a BSc, was a Corporate Member of the British Institute of Radio Engineers, had become a captain in the REME and held a first-class certificate as a teacher of the deaf, Manchester University. Six of our teachers had BA after their names. Two were holders of the National College of Teachers of the Deaf awards. Four were holders of the Manchester University Certificate for Teachers of the Deaf. Our school was strictly an 'oral school' from first to last, not just in the classrooms. And yet when the cat's away the mice do play: sign language appeared in one form or another *when authority* was absent! I did not use sign language as such, but I did gesture, as everyone in the world does! Being reprimanded by Mrs Askew for this on one single solitary occasion (despite my denials that I was not signing, but *gesturing*) lost me the yearly *speech* award!

Mr Askew, our new principal, was a grand fellow and I got along fine with him. He truly helped to make my four years (1949–53) at the Mary Hare Grammar School some of the absolutely happiest of my life. Yes, he was strict – overly at times – but he was fair-minded and knew an awful lot about people in general, not just deaf people. We corresponded quite regularly and interestingly up to the summer following my Churchill Fellowship. He was angered about what I wrote after witnessing the widespread use of sign language in America, where it is part and parcel of their lives. He sent me a sharp letter after reading a copy of the extract on signing (selected by a member of the Commonwealth Society for the Deaf), in which he mentioned he resented that those of us who had benefited from *pure oralism* were *casting it to the winds*. He felt that I, an oralist, and others of my ilk were denying oralism to others, which was not, and is not, true. It never has been on my part. I have always been a strong supporter of oralism *where it is feasible and I know it can be of great benefit to an individual deaf person*. My generation of deaf people know from our vast experience of life that we are part of the hearing world in our everyday lives. We know that *pure* oralism is *darned hard work.*

Your eyes are your ears from morning till night 365 days of every year of your life! Multiply that by the hours per year in which we conduct our waking lives and you may begin to appreciate the strain of *pure oralism*! When this is coupled with the strain and stress of working amongst all *hearing folk*, especially for those who are totally deaf, you may begin to appreciate the enormity and complexity of *pure oralism.*

Yes! *I* have undoubtedly benefited a hundredfold from pure oralism, *but I am not born deaf.* That entails a huge difference! Pure oralism educationally has been a *godsend to me personally*, enabling me to retain the speech I already had to a most high degree. I therefore do not have a *deaf voice*, as such! I am truly grateful for what oralism has done for *me.* Nevertheless it has not always been *easy.* As I grow older it becomes harder still to live with pure oralism. Like many of us enlightened ones, I do use sign language amongst other deaf people. Within my family we use gesturing or finger spelling (to a certain extent) if I have undue difficulty following a conversation. I have no hang-ups in relation to the *battle* between the theory and practice of *pure oralism and sign language.*

After years of struggling with my conscience, I'm at peace with myself on this account. However, I am perfectly and honestly able to go on record to champion *pure oralism* as an *ideal* goal! To contradict that, I would add *for whomsoever it is comfortably appropriate for.* We are all different human beings – some more capable than others. Think of us as a shop full of shoes of various sizes, colours, patterns, designs and *customers' tastes*! You should aim to fit the deaf person to the *shoe* which he or she is comfortable and content to *wear.*

From a *straw poll* of *educated* deaf people, the verdict is *total communication.* It is the logical answer.

Miss Mary Hare *opened up our lives* and all the *avenues and understandings* that were formerly closed to deaf people. Her *understanding and her vision and enlightenment* have enabled countless hundreds and thousands of us to become *ordinary human beings.*

How thrilled she would have been to know deaf people appear on television in their own programmes!

How thrilled she would be to know what wonderful families of our own we have raised.

How thrilled she would be to know that deaf people are now *an accepted minority* in the real world.

How thrilled she would be to know that deaf people are no longer shut away in institutions and mental homes for the rest of their natural lives.

How thrilled she would be to know that deaf people attend universities and colleges, are priests, accountants, teachers . . . *ad infinitum*.

How thrilled she would be to know that deaf people are no longer merely trained as cleaners, shoe repairers and launderers, which formerly were the main avenues of remunerative employment available and permissible to deaf persons – even to those of high calibre and education.

May the God Almighty in the heavens look with great kindliness and admiration upon Miss Mary Hare, Mr Mundin, Mr Askew, Miss Mitchell, Miss Brink, Mr Lee and all those other wonderful teachers who have departed this life, and on those still amongst us!

I, for one, never cease thanking them in my prayers. They were not saints – they had their mundane faults exactly like you and I. They were inspired, dedicated TEACHERS in the true sense and meaning of the word, to be looked up to! And – dare I enunciate it loudly? – RESPECTED! A respected teacher *earns that respect* and it makes teaching easier in the long run!

Many years after my children were born and growing up, myself and other former MHGS pupils attended the party for Mr Askew's retirement. There was a huge contingent of us, like one big happy family! Husbands, wives, children – we were all ready to show our respect if not our love to Mr Askew for his unselfish devotion to *our rights*, our education and our advancement as *human beings*! Under his *beady eye* we did him and his staff *proud*, becoming enduring symbols of well-educated adults and fine men and women, and good citizens of our country, which I still like to think of as Great Britain before the nineties' movement to fragment it!

I often smile at memories of a prefect telling me that Mr Askew *wanted to see me*! Wondering what I had copped for myself, I hastily went over in my head any possible misdemeanours. I stood outside his study door and knocked. The sign would light up: either '*engaged*', meaning someone was with him or he was on the telephone; or if it was OK to go in then the '*enter*' sign would flash up. To my relief he merely wanted me to stitch the end of his academic gown (which our teachers wore all day). He had a habit of striding like a whirlwind through the heavy ornate Manor House doors and his gown flowing with the force of the breeze his entry or exit entailed would catch on the handle and *rip*. Being handy with a needle I often hurriedly stitched the tears for him!

One day in Edgar Mundin Dormitory my room-mates and I were having a *heigh-ho* of a good time! From our huge windows we were able to *step out* on to a flat part of the roof of the conservatory. There down below on the newly fallen tantalising snow were some of the boys! Seeing us they yelled and threw snowballs. Ducking, we threw some back, but they were better shots than us!

Snowballs hit the windows, and as we tried *en masse* to scramble back inside through the bottom part of the windows well-aimed snowballs whizzed into our dormitory, spattering snowflakes on beds and on the highly polished flooring!

Attacked on the side facing the bowling lawn and the side facing the water garden and frozen fish pond, we tumbled giggling in a flurry of arms and legs on to the nearest beds! But the floor! Oh my!

Audrey and a few of the girls went back out again, opening the window ready for the affray and a fresh onslaught! In the excitement nobody thought of the *consequences*(!) or even to yell to the boys to *stop*. They would not have heard us anyway! Why waste our breath!

Audrey was fun! She had thick curly red hair and an ebullient nature. She was in her element!

Our bedroom was like fairyland, with slushy snowflakes spattering the walls. Not for nothing were our male school chums good bowlers at cricket!

The excitement and fun left us not knowing whether to laugh or cry! Miss Keates, our matron, had entered the room unheard and unseen! Her mouth was quivering and her eyes twinkling!

Hastily Audrey was dragged back inside the window. The recalcitrant occupiers of Edgar Mundin Dormitory stood looking sheepishly and hangdog at Miss Keates! Her quivering lips set firmly and she gave a huge sigh! Ominous!

The tirade poured forth about unladylike behaviour; she had thought better of us and been *wrong*! "Furthermore, girls, you can get some floor polish from Nellie the maid and repolish the whole floor by hand!"

"Can't we use Nellie's polishing machine?"

"No, you cannot. That is your punishment for behaving like street urchins!"

Out stalked Miss Keates! I'll wager she burst out laughing once we could not see her face!

Obtaining the necessary requisites, we removed our dark-green school tunics. Clad in our dark-green interlock pocketed knickers and thick beige-brown stockings held up by unattractive wide suspenders, we set to. We had no option! We took turns in sitting on the dusters and pushing and pulling one another over the floor until we could see our face in it! It was akin to the St Trinian's mob! White blouses, striped ties and dark-green drawers!

Undressed for the shower, one nameless girl(!) flung her garments on to her bedside chair. She returned smelling like a rose without a thorn in her dressing gown just in time, or rather too late! One of us had thrown her bra and girdle out of the window to the boys below! Fortunately they'd got caught on the ivy, or a projection! We formed a human chain with the first person leaning precariously three-quarters out of the window. Eventually the *objects* were recovered after much shouting and *words* which we couldn't hear and tried hard to see *from the distance*. Their gesturing and sign language was a little more understandable! But it was glorious fun.

Today, some children of the above-mentioned culprits may be surprised yet relieved to know that once upon a time we were *youngsters* and *young adults* who got up to pranks!

Fun is not the prerogative of the modern generation, no matter how much they think they have the edge on us!

There was a *grand* piano in the hall in the main Manor House and David M. was fond of *picking* out tunes on it; being partially deaf, he was quite adept. One time out of school hours I persuaded him to *try out* a favourite of mine (I had only been deaf three or four years): 'Believe Me If All Those Endearing Young Charms'.

He didn't know it, so I improvised with my *memories* of the song. Now, I am not exactly the Swedish Nightingale, Jenny Lind – her of the Edwardian days, or was it Victorian? I warbled away, pressed against the grand piano to help me *get the vibrations better*. After David had finally picked it up, to our satisfaction, after countless *repeats*, our principal (whose study was adjacent to the hall) flew out of his study, his gown billowing like a sailing ship! If we didn't cease forthwith *he* would tell us what he would do to our *endearing young charms*! Needless to say, we obliged and exited at a smart pace to the nearby common room!

At Mary Hare Grammar School we made the most of our

opportunities, helping one another and being helped by our teachers, inside *classroom hours* and outside. Some of the students were *stone deaf*, some born deaf, some partially deaf, some severely hard of hearing. We were a mixed bag. All had to be able to speak to a certain extent because it was strictly an oral school. The school had been founded on that precept, continued by the trustees and guardians of Miss Hare's bequest.

Without exception our teachers were *good sports*, always helpful, cheerful and kind. They had not long left the armed forces and were used to being in a *community of people*!

My favourite history was social economic British history, instilled into my class by Mr Bates, a new, young, good-looking teacher, newly married.

Miss Cragg, an older teacher, was the main history tutor and her favourite period was Charles I and II. Like the other single teachers she lived in the Manor House (married teachers had cottages close by). She was always *invading* the common room where we relaxed after our prep and supper. Out of earshot she went by the soubriquet of *Craggy*. One evening Craggy entered the common room to give us an uninvited and unexpected *lesson* in citizenship!

She had a newspaper spread from outstretched hand to hand; it was a broadsheet newspaper. She proceeded to discuss *happenings* in the paper with some of us. That was one of her merry ways of culturally *improving our minds*. She meant well, although it was customary for *only* the duty tutor to *invade our space*, in modern parlance. Her endeavours were met with good grace. She'd probably been lonely in her bed-sitting room and came down for a bit of company!

It did mean that horseplay was put on *hold* until she'd departed upstairs again.

Craggy's golden rule was, 'Read, digest, disseminate, sum up – to learn!' Not a bad precept.

In retrospect Craggy's *cultural* discussions were good lip-reading sessions and usually engendered impromptu debates which served our inquiring minds well. Being deaf we were not able to *overhear* chatter or the radio, so discussions like Craggy's were a good source of *input*.

Smiles would wreath our faces (or groans!) when somebody waved their arms frantically in the air with the cry of "Here Comes Craggy!"

One time David W. called out the usual – "H...C...C...!" – and added a succinct rider: "She's got her head buried in a newspaper – politics for supper!"

Craggy, it must be said, was very interested in politics in an age when the average man in the street never thought about it until the annual budget day!

Ralph, Dorothy, Anne-Marie and myself fell in love with Donald Peers' and Nat King Cole's singing – the heart-throb *pops* of our day before modern teenagers *took over*. Dorothy had *pretty good hearing* and Miss Cragg had encouraged our interest. She had a huge floor-standing radio (like a television!) in her bed-sitting room amongst stacks and piles of books, newspapers and magazines! I think I have *inherited* her tendency to hoard anything made from paper!

At this particular time, once a week, Craggy would make herself *scarce* somewhere or other, leaving us alone in her room with our ears or microphones of body hearing aids literally against the huge loudspeaker of the radio! We had a cup of coffee each. We were very good: we touched nothing in her room apart from the radio. She trusted us – it was only about half an hour each week. We were so excited! With the radio at *full volume* (that's why she left us on our own!) we listened dreamily (as much as our ears permitted) to the magical refrains of 'In A Shady Nook by a Babbling Brook' and 'There's a Strawberry Moon in a Blueberry Sky'. Miss Cragg had taken the time and trouble to give us a music sheet with the words on, so we followed the beat!

I don't think Craggy appreciated us as much as we appreciated her!

A pile of old and *modern* records turned up in the common room from *somewhere*. Mr Bates had written the refrains of some of the songs for us, in his own spare time.

At school it was customary to rise early in the week with an extra hour's lie-in on Sundays, unless you were going by bicycle to the half-hour (no hymns) Holy Communion at church (before breakfast). At this time there was a *favourite record* called 'Goodnight, Sweetheart'. (At present it is enjoying a revival with a television programme of the same title on BBC.) Being serenaded at the *unearthly hour* of 7 a.m. morning after morning with the same record was just a bit too much for Craggy! She fair blew her top: storming into the common room in her dressing gown, metal Dinkie curlers and face cream! For a whole month we were banned

145

from playing 'Goodnight, Sweetheart' at seven in the morning. Which was a shame! Early morning was the daily *snogging time* for the boys and girls – they got up at six! The records were their *obvious* excuse!

Poor Miss Cragg! Being deaf and deafened, we didn't have a clue how loud the record was! The machine, which was cranked energetically by a handle, was on full power!

In middle life Craggy inferred that *anybody could do anything if they tried hard enough*. Practising what she preached, Craggy took driving lessons and piano lessons. Whether she was a *beginner* or on refreshers I cannot say. She *plonked the grand piano in the hall*, if not with the Liberace touch, with verve and vigour. After school hours, hell-bent on *culture*, she thought nothing of marshalling us like a brood of chicks around the grand piano. We were too polite to resist! Our generation did what it was told, more or less! Craggy's face beamed like a lighthouse, full of joy and goodness. She placed us into a certain order! The better-hearing ones were at the back of our small group, the mediums with hearing aids in the middle and the totally deaf leaning against the grand piano to better feel the vibrations. Our eyes glued to her face, we followed her *singing* and her breathing techniques. It truly was great wholesome fun! We went through the whole mixed bag from 'Polly Wolly Doodle', 'The Battle Hymn of the Republic' and 'Knick Knack Paddy Wack' (a favourite of hers) to a current hit song, 'Sweet Violets'. The boys mockingly in true barbershop style would make exaggerated mouth movements, hand on heart, because my name is Violet!

I had two fun names at school: Flying Elephant, because I was a hefty girl, and Grandma Vie, because I was for ever stitching the torn blazer pockets of the boys, so Matron would not tick them off!

The boys usually tore their blazers in mock wrestling matches in the common room. It was *de rigueur* for boys to wear their blazers indoors. Not so for the girls. Evidently unisex had not then reared its somewhat unlovely head.

Down on the lacrosse field one day somebody threw the ball so swiftly and unexpectedly it literally knocked out one of the front teeth of one of the more senior girls. Luckily it passed through her the following morning in the privacy of the lavatories. Nature has its own ways!

Inside and outside of school hours we were a veritable hive of activity. The devil would have been hard put to find work for idle hands. We were all up to something nearly all the time! Various clubs abounded on the school premises: Drama Club, Library Club, Social Committee, Pig Club, Beekeeping Association, Chinchilla Club, Billiards Club, Photographic Club, Table Tennis Club ... We played football, tennis, stoolball, cricket, rounders, lacrosse and hockey and went swimming in Newbury. There was a Girl Guide troop (I was in Kingfisher) and a Scout troop and we had ballroom-dancing lessons. Irene went horse riding and was in gymkhanas, which some of us attended to cheer her on!

The Pig Club members held shares in it and they raised twelve healthy piglets, selling eight at £5 each and keeping for breeding purposes and store two hogs and two gilts. At various ages they sold for anything up to £25 each.

The Pig Club had been started in 1951 with Mr Askew as chairman, Geoffrey as vice-chairman and Jack as the honorary treasurer. On Cup Final day they had set out determined to purchase two large white pigs! They did return with two, but not large nor white! It had been suggested that the piggies could be named after the first two goalscorers in the Cup Final, but they couldn't both be called Jackie Milburn! Both piggies turned out to be female! A name-the-pig competition was set into action at one penny per entry in old money. The prize was a five-shilling (25p) share in the Pig Club. Alison and Anne won and shared the prize. To finance the club 100 similar shares were printed, which quickly sold out inside the school. Bubble and Squeak, the two piggies, had a magnificent sty built for them by Geoffrey, David and Jack with the help of some old iron gates left by the builders; a daily rota for cleaning *Their Majesties* was drawn up. There was plenty of kitchen waste to feed their piggy appetites. Each pig was insured against *premature death*!

The Pig Club flourished long after we were gone. By 1962 they had thirty-seven blue piglets, two Wessex saddleback sows, two large white sows, two blue sows and a large white boar. Who was it said that *big trees from little acorns grow*?

The Beekeeping Club (which I was in) was another lucrative business. We sold the honey to the school at a profit. Mr Askew loaned me his old army trousers for beekeeping! I had none in my sparse wardrobe. (Most females wore dresses or skirts in those days.) Mr Askew was over six feet and I was five feet one and a half inches! (I am four feet five inches in 2018!) An old hat of his covered with a bit of tatty netting kept the bees off my face. I wore Mr Askew's thick gloves (my hands are tiny, size 6!) and my socks tucked into my wellies – not quite *haute couture*, but eminently sensible.

Poor red-headed Audrey. Her face netting had a rather big hole and the bees got through it! She was terribly stung on her poor little face. It was frightening to see and she was awfully ill. Her face swelled like an enormous scarlet dumpling, her eyes looking like two black currants.

Eventually she did recover, but she was on bed rest for quite some time. We were all very worried about her. I did not want to experience a similar fate and it put me off beekeeping for life! I had enjoyed using the smoke guns to get the bees off the honeycombs to remove the excess bee nest of the interloper queen. Only one queen bee was allowed. The idea was that the smoke would induce passiveness in the busy little industrious bees going about their lawful business. Unfortunately poor Audrey's hive of bees had not become *tiddly enough*!

I told you our tutors (male) had been captains in the armed forces. My husband, when he was alive, always averred that I was *so precise* about certain things. "Why do you have to be so precise?" The military skills of our tutors rubbed off on us!

Before breakfast each morning we stripped our beds fully to air the mattresses, and opened the windows summer and winter. After breakfast we remade them and tidied the dormitory. The wide tip of the sheet the hem side had to be turned downwards. Blankets were mitred and bedspreads half-mitred. Pillows were placed with the open end away from a window or door. Prefects inspected each morning and if they were not satisfied they made you strip and remake your bed. Ingrained habits die hard and I still follow this procedure, even with modern duvets!

Our school Girl Guide troop was the 10th Newbury Company and Miss Gardiner was our Guide Captain. I was in Kingfisher Patrol. Miss Gardiner was the school's longest-ever serving teacher.

Guide meetings were held in the lofts of the outbuildings, but we soon had to find other venues. The buildings were being altered as flats for the domestic staff. Fire lighting, tent pitching, gadget making, bed making, cooking and sleeping in tents out of doors used all our surplus energy.

One weekend, Jean Goadsby, Jean Smith, Joan Godfrey and myself were camping out alone in the school grounds. The weather was glorious and the surrounding fields and hedges of the school's extensive grounds kept us safe from prying eyes. Our washing-up bowl was wedged into a tripod of sticks – part of our gadget-making test! Wearing swimming costumes (quite modest by modern

148

standards), we were bashfully interrupted when the smiling face of Alan Taylor appeared before us!

After the initial shock we all took turns taking photos, which was a daring thing to do in our *cossies*!

After Alan had gone we got ready for the night. The midges in the tent bothered us something awful. Jean crawled round the *pup* tent with a large half-bottle of Dettol disinfectant which Matron had loaned us. One by one the midges met their nemesis. Matron never saw that half-bottle of Dettol again and we had some explaining to do!

On one occasion my spectacles frame broke. I never had the money to get new ones: I was seventeen years old. I couldn't write home for money! Mr Askew, ever resourceful, came to my rescue with an old dark-brown pair of his. He removed his lenses and stuck mine in their place – problem solved (see photo, page 87).

I remember in May 1951 we had a half-term holiday. Those who lived a long way away – like Scotland, for example – went to stay with friends. Father said I could not go home because he did not want to pay my fare or feed me! An unknown benefactor, a teacher, offered to pay my fare. Mr Askew wrote and informed my parents. Father sent a sarcastic letter back to Mr Askew saying he did not want me home to feed me! I only lived in Dagenham! It wasn't far away. Mr Askew said Father should have been shot and wished he could do it himself! I was the only girl with some boys left at school for half-term. Miss Keates, the matron, turned the sickbay into a lovely sitting room with a bowl of flowers. For a whole week I had my meals alone with Miss Keates and I was very spoilt. Mr Askew arranged outings for us, and one of them was to the South Bank in London to the Festival of Britain.

Mr Shirley, when he took the seniors at a later date, pinned this notice on the noticeboard.

BATTLE ORDERS FOR THE FOURTH COMPANY
THE MARY HARE LIGHT INFANTRY

1.   10.30 a.m.   March to South Bank (storm barrier at all cost).
2.   Mass Attack on Dome of Discovery.
3.   Disperse to Attack Enemy from All Quarters.
4.   14.55   Reassemble Under Skylon to Count Casualties.
5.   15.00   General Withdrawal.

The Festival of Britain celebrated the centenary of the Great Exhibition of 1851 with four main exhibitions and a pleasure garden at Battersea Park. The main display was on the South Bank between Waterloo and Westminster Bridge – a site of twenty-seven acres. The Dome of Discovery was 365 feet in diameter, with the largest unsupported roof in the world. The whole site had been a derelict area. The Festival Hall is still standing today. Many pavilions abounded and were of great diverse interest: 'The Land of Britain', 'Minerals of the Islands', 'The Country of Natural Scenes', 'Sea, Ships and Transport' and 'Power and Production'. There were exhibits on the seaside, British traditions, homes and gardens, schools and health. There were restaurants and shows. The riverside was gaily decorated with flags and colourful bunting. In one place The Lion and the Unicorn Pavilion had beautiful fat white artificial doves of peace hanging suspended from the roof.

I was doubly fortunate because I again visited the exhibition at a later date with the rest of the seniors.

Round about this time Miss Chapman was in charge of the menus at school; suddenly they became inordinately bountiful (we always ate well before that) and made a welcome change. Unfortunately they coincided with a slimming craze running rampant amongst the female species at the Manor House. The boys were extra-helpful, managing to eat our too bountiful share as well as their own. There were no complaints to Miss Chapman, and the boys were congratulated on their generosity of spirit!

The School of Military Survey (Army) was at Hermitage, near our school. It was with much anticipated excitement and trepidation that we girls joined the boys on the *geographical* visit to the camp. Our first chance to attempt our feminine wiles on the military! Church visits on certain Sundays hereafter became quite an event! We watched the soldiers marching into church and took the opportunity to wave and smile at them! We had high hopes of appealing to their manhood. A military uniform does put gloss on a man!

During my time at Mary Hare Grammar School, conscription into the armed forces was still compulsory in Britain. Our male students aged eighteen were automatically obliged to *sign up* when they received their calling-up papers. It was a hilarious giggle, for the boys knew they would fail their medical *because of deafness*. They strutted around, preening themselves, giving wry imaginary *interviews*, causing the girls to fall about laughing hysterically.

Well, laughter is contagious!

This went until 4 December 1952, when Alan Taylor travelled to Brookwood from Birmingham with other *conscripts* for national service. Alan had, of course, previously signed up like the other boys of his age, expecting to be automatically turned down. The MO must have had a drop too much, for he actually passed Alan for the RAOC! Alan was partially deaf and a gentle fellow. He was herded into a big army lorry and sent off with the others, who had passed their medicals. They'd gone in and out of army huts with kit thrown at them and a hurried medical! Some of the lads were dressed like spivs! After one week's training Alan was *footsore*. The Corporal was nastily sarcastic. When the Sergeant Major roared, "Left turn!" poor Alan turned *right*! He was a *hindrance to others* at drill: he could not understand the commands shouted *out on the parade ground*! (There were no modern post-aural hearing aids.)

Alan was put to work in the stores, and at the end of January he was *honourably discharged*, much to his and our school's relief!

CHAPTER THIRTEEN

Every week for four years Mother faithfully sent my five shillings (25p) pocket money. Half a crown was from Mother and the rest was made up from the housekeeping which the girls gave her. Emmie, Tiny, Queenie and Eileen were married by the time I left school. Thelma of course had died.

Mother was not much of a scholar as regards writing letters. All I got in the way of *news* from home was the postal order and a scrap of paper torn off a larger sheet which said, 'Dear Vie, Here is your pocket money, love from Mum.' Not very enlightening! (Every week the same few words.)

There was a school bank, and we each had our own chequebook. Every week we would line up in the main hall of the Manor House with whatever we wanted to draw out written on a cheque and counterfoil. The banker, a teacher, would look at the cheque. If we wanted more than half a crown (12½p) we had to give a special reason *why*. This small amount of money was a fair bit (as spending money went) in those days. I bought sweets, writing paper, envelopes and maybe talcum powder or a sachet of shampoo powder from Woolworth's, which was our Mecca each Saturday.

We would spend part of Saturday mornings in there agonising over exactly what we were going to purchase. I often had my eye on a small bottle of Evening in Paris perfume, in its distinctive dark-blue bottle. I cannot recall actually purchasing it, but may have done once in a while. The sachet of shampoo was maybe about a penny halfpenny or twopence in old money.

Woolworth's was cheap in those far-off days. Apart from Saturday shopping, the town of Newbury was *out of bounds* to us unless there was a special reason to go there. We had a cup of tea and a cake in the Bandalog Café above a shop. We thought we were being very adult and sophisticated *like hearing people* because we were doing *ordinary things!*

It was strictly forbidden to even eat an ice cream in the streets of Newbury! If a prefect saw you there was hell to pay and a meeting with the principal on the following Monday. I don't recall any of our lot *tempting fate.*

One Saturday we were walking past a record shop whose door was wide open and Dorothy (partially hearing) dragged us in to *hear* some music! Anne-Marie (partially hearing) agreed it was *smashing!* I put my ear close to the sound and felt the vibrations on my cheek, to the shopkeeper's amusement, and agreed it was *smashing!* (Our hearing aids were at school. They were huge and cumbersome and worn in a leather satchel.) We would have *died* rather than be seen wearing the old Medresco National Health hearing aids out of doors! Well, we were at a young, self-conscious age! Dorothy made me and Anne-Marie promise to back her onslaught on Miss Cragg to purchase the record when we met at the next social-services meeting. The record was Nat King Cole singing 'They Try to Tell Us We're Too Young'.

We told Craggy. She seemed dubious, not sure if it was culturally correct for us, but promised to go into town and listen to it and judge for herself. After much discussion Miss Cragg decided the record would not *corrupt us* and it was duly purchased. She went one better and wrote down the lyrics for us so that we could follow the beat of the sound and the inflexion of Cole's beautiful voice. Usually, if we knew what was being played and we listened with Medresco aids at the very beginning, then with the words in front of us, we could, after a fashion, follow the song. A lot of times it was intelligent guesswork, but we became adept at *guessing* as I still am today! For my part I cannot today hear consonants – only vowel sounds with my hearing aid and nothing without! My hearing deteriorated yearly. By 2018 it is now 115–120 decibels in my right ear. So life is still very much intelligent guesswork and lip-reading.

Mr Barrett gave us singing lessons! Yes! With his deep big voice and gestures akin to André Previn and Daniel Barenboim combined we got a good *grounding* in singing! How his ears and that of the other teachers managed to *stomach it* I shall never know.

He would stand some few yards from us, inhale and exhale showing us what he wanted to see come from each of us! He must have been an incurable optimist. It was not the norm to teach deaf people to sing or *listen* to music then.

He was a great stickler for pronunciation of the beginnings and endings of words when singing!

He would tell us to *almost* start the next line of a song with the end of the word we had just finished! He was a good tutor, with endless patience, and we had many a laugh with Mr Barrett. We were not in line to become Maria Callas or, one of my favourites, Joseph Locke (of 'Hear My Song, Violetta'): but we did our very best to learn! I think Miss Cragg's friendly impromptu sessions were more fun though.

My tutors helped me and others with our speech with a selfless dedication that often went beyond the call of paid duty. But then, that is what *real teachers do*, isn't it!

Mr Shirley was a kindly harmless dear fellow. He was something like an eccentric boffin, but he knew his onions! He was a marvellously brilliant teacher of English; and if you're listening up in heaven, Mr Shirley, I'd like you to know I still practise what you preached. He carried a little book with him and each time he came across unfamiliar words he would jot them down in his little notebook and in his spare time look them up in his dictionary. I still do that! There are a tremendous number of words in our vocabulary – especially today, with new ones springing up almost overnight! Words change and often meanings change.

I recall an interesting interview on television with the dead Duke of Windsor, and the interviewer was asking him what he thought of miniskirts (in the miniskirt era). The Duke of Windsor dated himself immediately by saying they were all right provided they wore the correct *underpinnings*, meaning underwear!

Look at the word 'loo', which does not mean the card game of loo, but toilet. That has undergone a change from lavatory and water closet or WC to loo! And to be as gay as a lark – the meaning of the word gay has changed. Mr Shirley instilled in us the changing nature of words.

Mr Shirley made English come to life. Mesmerised we eyed him like a hawk as Shakespeare's *Macbeth* cascaded in torrents from his mouth. I can still quote parts of *Macbeth* today!

Whenever I think of *Macbeth* as a play I think of poor Mr Shirley. Tragically he died not long after of something *rare*, leaving a wife and two young sons. I guess he is up there helping the angels with their diction and Shakespeare!

Before Mr Shirley, Miss Gardiner was our splendid English teacher (our form). Audrey was quite carried away by her recitation of 'The Highwayman' by Alfred Noyes. Audrey, who is stone deaf, used to say, "Alfred No Yes"! She knew how to say it correctly, but found it fun to tease with it as "No Yes". We all called it the same after Audrey started the *craze*. I admired Audrey. With her glorious abundant rich red hair she had *a helluva quick temper*, but it passed over as quickly as it came! She was great fun to know. We were in the same dormitories and classrooms all the time we were at Mary Hare Grammar School. She lost all her hearing at five years of age. She managed to speak extraordinarily well. Her great love was dancing and again she achieved all that she set out to do. After school she married Ronald, another pupil who had no hearing, and they settled down at Shaw in Newbury with two lovely children. They now have gorgeous grandchildren and are much loved by their family. Sadly Audrey is not well now. It is heartbreaking to see her because she was so vivacious and alive. She teased Mr Shirley, but he took it in good stead for she was a fellow thespian and loved poetry. [1]Audrey adored dancing. Her sense of rhythm and the beat was second to none. Ballroom dancing and dramatics, aside from poetry, were her great loves. I always recall Audrey, not just because we were in the same dormitories and classrooms but because of her jolly exuberance of life.

She played the wicked stepmother in the school's production of *Snow White and the Seven Dwarfs*. Miss Gardiner, another of our brilliant English teachers, arranged it and Mrs Askew choreographed and directed the music *action*. Eleanor played Snow White. She was lovely. Mrs Askew arranged a *hidden background* chorus of partially deaf and profoundly deaf students to sing the *music* whilst Eleanor danced and mimed the words (lip-reading Mrs Askew to keep in time) of 'I'm Wishing' and 'Someday My Prince Will Come'. It was so beautiful it remains locked in my memory banks. The prancing *horses* were a line-up of girls doing a stepping prance in time to music, relying on Mrs Askew at the corner of the stage to visibly count the beat of the rhythm with her pointed finger to keep them in step. Eleanor and Graham were wonderful at Scottish reels, in which Mrs Askew coached both of them. Alison, partially deaf, sweet and shy, did a magnificent Lady Macbeth. Her interpretation of *out damned spot* sent shivers down our spines! Ronald was the physician, and little things like

---

1 *Audrey died a few years ago with Pick's disease*

that stick in one's memory. Alison later went to Oxford University and became a qualified librarian, amongst her other achievements.

It was Audrey who coined the phrase 'Can't tell talk from splutter'! (Difficulty in lip-reading.)

One of our younger teachers was Mr Bates, whom I briefly mentioned. He later became headmaster of Bolton School for the Deaf. I may be wrong, but to the best of my memory Arnold Bates came to see the Mary Hare Grammar School with a party of graduate teachers. Impressed and intrigued, he became a teacher of the deaf and introduced British economic history to us: he really brought it alive. He was an excellent teacher with a lovely wife.

Mr Brown was the Scout troop's Scoutmaster and Mr Bates his assistant. Mr Bates also took up hard-court and lawn tennis. When he married we gave the happy couple Pyrex dishes (the first I had ever seen). When Mrs Bates went to evening classes to learn cookery we asked Mr Bates how his wife was getting on. His rugged face crinkled into a naughty grin as he said, "Fine! She only burns one side of the toast now."

Mr Hill, another teacher, was another whom Audrey delighted in teasing; we all did! Audrey nicked his pen out of his front breast pocket and nipped up the side staircase one flight above the boy's bedrooms. She stood there holding out his pen cheekily, knowing he was not allowed to follow her on to the girls' floor. He took it all in good part and Audrey finally relented and dropped his pen to him!

Before I moved to Norfolk I dropped in at the Old Kent Road School in London and Mr Hill was the headmaster. He chuckled as he remembered Audrey and his fountain pen, and he gave me a warm welcome.

Miss Hall taught French. She was a most petite dainty little lady, probably a size 8! She was English, but her subject was French. When she walked into our classrooms the boys sighed heavily with great emphasis, placing their hands over their hearts and gazing at her with lovelorn looks! Poor, poor Miss Hall! She went bright scarlet and rushed out of the room. After a few minutes she'd reappear again and the boys would be sitting quietly and attentively on their best behaviour! It happened each and every French lesson! The boys would not have hurt her for the world. They loved her, even though most of us never loved French verbs and adverbs and feminine and masculine words! Miss Hall was a good sport! I managed to learn that *Toto est dans la salle à manger*!

Alan's repertoire of French extended only as far as *le bris*! He was a big, gentle lad and towered above petite Miss Hall.

Our days began early. If we didn't wake ourselves up, Matron would give us a push and pull the bedclothes back. We could not have heard a *rising bell*, of course. After a cooked breakfast there was the assembly in the main hall, which by the law of our country followed a religious pattern, with prayers, hymns and daily readings from a lectern by one of the prefects, or by the current head girl or head boy. Ross and David H. (we had a lot of boys with the name of David) were excused the religious part and so was Ruth because they were of the Jewish faith. When we had religious knowledge at school they were excused that particular class. When we went to the Church of England they were excused that too and it never caused any undue problems as far as I am aware. The Catholics went to the Catholic church. We were a family, no matter our beliefs: we treated each other on equal terms. At assembly the principal would give his pep talk or tell us who'd been naughty, as principals have always done down the centuries! Everyone, no matter their faith, was included in the principal's talk.

After that we would go to our groups for speech lessons for half an hour each morning. Lessons were followed by a compulsory siesta on our beds. We could sleep or read, but not chatter to one another, but we did! The duty prefect walked around checking on us. The siesta was after lunch and was to help us rest from the stress of lip-reading lessons with pure oralism. It is hard lip-reading Shakespeare and French – you try it with your ears plugged up!

More lessons followed in the afternoon, then for a short period before teatime there were compulsory games (not fixtures – they were on specified days), which could include, amongst others, practice at football, cricket in the cricket nets, lacrosse, stoolball or rounders: our *surplus* energy was healthily *soaked up*! Rain, snow, sun or slight fog, we still had our daily *games*, ending with hot showers before teatime. At one time it can be said, only as an experiment, we girls were initiated into the art of playing cricket! I do not think we were very good at it!

On Saturday mornings time was found for the girls to darn their brown *Nora Batty*-style stockings (mine eventually had more darns in the heels than actual stocking!) or to wash a few smalls, although the bulk of our laundry went into large laundry baskets (like huge picnic baskets) which were *sent out* to a commercial laundry. When it came back Matron sorted it via our sewed-in Cash's name tapes and left our clean clothes on the ends of our beds. Then we had to place them in our respective drawers.

Matron was a stickler for *tidy drawers* and inspected the contents *without warning!* For the girls, it was one pair of dark green bloomers on, one pair in the laundry and one pair in the drawers, and ditto for the rest of our school clothes and regulation underwear. That was why we were always rinsing our knickers and drying them illicitly on the hot pipes in the washroom or domestic-science room!

In the *covered way* there was an old-fashioned kind of glass-topped *lean-to* which joined some of the building to the main Manor House. Matron or (usually) her deputy would inspect our shoes, and the compulsory brown leather sandals which were worn on the premises. Shoes were not permitted on the premises on weekdays – only on Saturday or Sunday evenings or special occasions. Rubber-soled sandals were normally worn by the boys and girls.

If the shoes or sandals required repairing the toe or toe and heel or the whole sole would be marked with a heavy chalked cross and then they were tossed into a huge wicker basket, which was sent off to a *cobbler*. Our names were written inside our shoes, just like everything else was labelled.

During my time at Mary Hare Grammar School there was more than one matron; we got along fine with all of them. Girls or boys could discuss their little *problems* and be assured of a sympathetic ear. Matron and her deputy were our *mums in loco parentis*.

Many an older girl (about sixteen to nineteen years) went to Matron complaining about their *hairstyles* being ruined during compulsory games in slightly inclement weather! Hairdryers and the hot curlers of modern times were not part of our lifestyle! Girls who had straight hair went through agonies of *sleeping in uncomfortable metal Dinkie curlers* or *rags*; they did not take kindly to having their *nightly suffering* spoilt on a wet and windy games field!

Often if they were particular lucky at any one time they could get away with a scarf tied round their heads! But not that often – it depended what mood the supervising teacher happened to be in!

Eric Brown was our geography teacher, somewhat dapper like the late film star David Niven. He'd been a captain in the King's army and he had a most charming wife, who was an ex-nurse. With their beautiful little daughter, Christine, they were an acceptable part of our social lives as well as our school lives. Mr Brown always seemed to be smiling! He finally left our school to become the headmaster at a school for the deaf in Middlesex, yet kept in touch by attending many special occasions and some reunion dinners and dances.

To the boys' delight, Mr Brown invariably incorporated into our geography lessons some of his *army life*: manoeuvres, tactics and very interesting anecdotes of *wartime army style*. Possibly not *de rigueur*, but he made his geography lessons come to life. However, on reflection and in retrospect, I was not much good at geography *textbook style* and remain one of the world's worst map readers! No reflection on Mr Brown's teaching, it's just that I am a bit thick when it comes to map reading today! I was never able to master it in the Girl Guides either!

Mr Salt, another teacher, and his pretty wife were favourites of mine. They had three children, Malcolm, Rosemary and the baby, Catherine, and they lived in one of the school outbuildings, the Bothy, a delightful cottage. Many happy hours of mine were spent with Mrs Salt, who taught some of us smocking and gave me and other students sandwiches and lemonade in the small cottage living room. One day Mrs Salt rushed us all outside and pointed to the sky. It was a low-flying aeroplane piloted by Mr Salt himself. He flew as low as he dared and dipped his wings in salute and we cheered and waved like mad!

During the Second World War Mr Salt had flown bombers and was awarded the DFC and AFC. When he left our school we heard that he was going to become a headmaster at Ballarat in Australia. On 25 November 1993 on page twelve of the *Daily Mail* there was a photo and story of a Dennis Salt of the wartime RAF, and I think it was our Mr Salt. His Halifax had been brought down on a raid at Stuttgart. But I'm not sure if it was him.

To give Mr and Mrs Salt a *break* I used to take the three children for a walk on Sundays. Baby Catherine lay in her pram chuckling away and her little legs kicking with delight. She adored going out in the pram and looking up at the leafy trees. Malcolm and Rosemary held the pram handle and off we went down by the Home Farm and up the long private lane which led to another lane and out from the Manor House. We could smell *our pigs* before we got far from the Bothy! They were not on the Home Farm, but had their *home* closer to the Manor House. The two older children and I would hold our noses in mock disgust and see who could pull the most horrible face! Another game we played, before we ventured on to the public highway and its verdant banks full of wild primroses, violets and other plants by the thousands, was *who's afraid of the big bad wolf?* I introduced this one to the children and it was their *very favourite*. The baby, Catherine, and I went on ahead slightly and little slim Rosemary and chunkier Malcolm danced along behind us at arm's length; I never let them get too far behind me because I was responsible for all three children!

They were very bright children and Malcolm was for ever stating that he was going to be a fire-engine driver when he grew up! His dad had told him that he could be whatever he wanted to be! I did hear a *rumour* that all three children had become teachers in adult life, but I never managed to verify that. I would love to know how they have got on in life.

CHAPTER FOURTEEN

Craggy decided one day that we *older ones* should form the nucleus of a Library Committee. Under her *chaperonage* we had special permission to go into the town of Newbury to *look at some suitable books*, ostensibly for weeding out whatever was not *quite right* for our young minds! At that particular time (1951) *The Cruel Sea* by Nicholas Monsarrat was all the rage. Craggy decided we were *too innocent* to peruse such a book let alone add it to the school library! (I laugh when I think today how tame that was compared to what is now seen and heard in print or on television!) By 1953 the book had been reprinted thirteen times! After much *democratic* discussion round the table, back at school, Miss Cragg finally agreed to purchase it for our library, but decreed it to be *too meaty for the under-sixteens*!

The age group at our school was eleven to nineteen, co-educational.

Indoors we had many activities besides the numerous clubs which abounded; I cannot recall ever *being bored*, which is the watchcry of today's young teenagers. Table tennis, darts, country-and-western dancing, skittles, silent film shows, shove-ha'penny, ping-pong. . . . We enjoyed a seemingly almost endless list of activities. For the boys wrestling was a number-one pastime, cheered on by us girls!

Towards the end of my time at Mary Hare Grammar School television came into existence at our school, but it was not at all popular! Black-and-white sets in a darkened room and no subtitles! Most of us did not like sitting in a darkened room – not unless one was snogging, and not even then sometimes. It was too difficult to communicate *orally* in a room like that! We couldn't lip-read one another in darkness!

There was only one channel – BBC – and McDonald Hobley was the main presenter wearing his *tuxedo*. Television was only broadcast at certain times in the evening and there were more exciting things to do than trying to lip-read a *miniature mouth* on a black-and-white screen. No! The attraction was *not yet* there for us! We were requested to give an *opinion* of Jasmine Bligh, who was another presenter, and I remember saying in my *written report* that 'It might be easier to lip-read her in black and white if she wore darker lipstick'!

Saturday night, whilst not quite Saturday-night fever, was nevertheless, in those far-off halcyon days of my youth, *the* night of the week for us pupils. On Saturday nights we wore mufti: skirt and blouse or jumper for girls (the boys usually just wore their Sunday grey suits, part of their uniform). We were, if over seventeen, permitted to wear *light make-up*. Being an avid *helper* and member of the Social Committee, I adored Saturday-night *arrangements* and indeed was awarded the Social Services Prize one year.

Social work has always come easy to me. I love people, I really do. The Social Committee meetings were a highlight of my spare time, when we plotted and planned ahead for the term's *Saturday-night socialising*. I say it was spare time, but actually our time was so well used up I don't think many of us *knew* what spare time was! School was like a hive of busy bees. I painted and designed the wall posters for the 'Coming attractions' of the Social Committee for each term of that particular year.

I was pleasantly pleased when they attracted large viewing audiences round the noticeboard, especially when certain posters announced some particular *thing* which they had to turn up at to actually find out what was going to happen on that particular Saturday night! All the bribes and offers of sweets or a bit of chocolate never prised the information from the Social Committee members. Our lips were sealed! And no, I would not oblige one persistent boy when he said I could whisper into his hearing aid behind cupped hands *so nobody else could lip-read me*!

My poster for the silent film *The Cat and the Canary* frightened some of the girls, who had to be persuaded by their current boyfriend it would be OK as they would be sitting next to them and holding their hand!

Today, I wish I had all those old posters!

Besides country-and-western dancing, where I stood on

a convenient chair next to the huge wind-up gramophone as the *caller*, waving my arms and pointing out the *moves* (from memory!) of the dancing, we had other friendly games, including whist drives, beetle drives, housey-housey (or bingo to you), darts tournaments and table-tennis ones, all between the four houses of the school – Thomas Arnold (red), Mary Hare (green), Thomas Braidwood (blue) and St John of Beverley (yellow). Conducting the country-and-western square-dancing and the Paul Jones medley I wore the old-fashioned satchel (NHS Medresco hearing aid) slung across my chest from one shoulder with the huge bicycle-style batteries in the heavy leather satchel.

The microphone was like a dance-hall one but with two leads, one from the top and one from the bottom, leading a few feet long to the earplug in my ear. Earplugs were not so small and discreet as modern ones; they stuck out!

Whenever I *lost* the beat, which was often, the duty teacher, like a guardian angel, would pop up from nowhere to set me right and then just disappear again! Well, the gramophone was on full blast! Mr Brown used to stick his finger in his ears and wiggle them frantically before he exited! The dancers, who would be waiting breathlessly for my flapping arms and mouth movements (to begin again), would heave sighs of relief and trip away to my directions! They didn't wear their hearing aids all the time – none of us did unless compelled to in the classrooms. And there I must confess that many of the boys *cheated*! They gave the impression of wearing aids, but it was just that, an impression! They pretended the batteries were in their pockets, plugged the earpiece into their ear and let the long lead disappear ostensibly to the batteries in a top pocket, but actually they did not have the batteries!

I don't think they were ever caught out; or else teachers turned a *blind eye*!

The girls of course were not *full of pockets*. We did not like the aids because they were heavy and, most importantly, the feedback, the whistling, was enough to drive a person potty. But, in time, one became acclimatised to them and they were a wonderfully well-powered hearing aid. It was just that they were so conspicuous! Today the young think nothing of wearing their Sony Walkman leads and radio in public, but we *did mind* because it labelled us! They were a great asset at assemblies and concerts and sing-songs round the piano. As hearing aids go in relation to technology they were of the best of their time. And they were available on the NHS.

Sometimes Mrs Askew, who was an ardent dancer of Scottish dances, would come and help us in her own free time. We must have *blasted her ears away*.

The powers that be decreed ballroom dancing! Miss Brookes, a magnificent tall specimen of long, lean womanhood oozing litheness and personality, entered the world of us older students. Her subject was ballroom dancing. She was determined we would be a credit to her and her teaching. Once a week *in our spare time* Miss Brookes came to teach us the rudiments, the poise, the skill and the pleasure of *real* ballroom dancing. She made the girls stand in a line across one end of the hall and the boys likewise at the other end. It was hilarious, with Miss Brookes in the middle of the room showing us alternately the man's steps and the lady's steps. The girls had to turn round and dance backwards, and it was quite a twisting feat on our part to keep our heads swivelled to follow her! We just had the old floor-standing wind-up gramophone from our *Saturday-night fever*! It used to wind down, and Miss Brookes hastily delegated certain boys to take it in turns to stay there and rewind quickly whenever her eagle eye beamed in on them! We did not just get our dark-green bloomers in a twist; our aching eyeballs became almost permanently twisted in their sockets and we diligently twisted our *unaccustomed dancing feet* to the ballroom steps, which were executed brilliantly, effortlessly, by Miss Brooke. She was at least six feet tall. We would politely, heroically, rise on tiptoe, skip a little step and try hard to please her. She was a *real brick* and had us in stitches! One time, to demonstrate how she wanted the boys to hold us – cue beetroot faces from the *boys* – she grabbed David W. (and he was about up to her chest!) in a close embrace to her bosom. He was wishing the floor would sink beneath him and take him with it, but he manfully attempted the steps she had taught us! Seeing his poor head on line with her bosom and not even a piece of paper possible to go between them the rest of us just folded up in hysterics, falling all over the place to the detriment of our dancing feet!

Seasonal activities, then, were the highlight of our school calendar. Each year we drew lots to decide which *house* (green, blue, red or yellow) was to host which of the four main parties of the year. We always had a cracking time and each housemaster or mistress tried to outdo the previous *planner's* contribution.

In our school there existed friendly rivalry amongst the houses, points being scored for diverse activities, culminating with the award at the end of each year for the *best house*. Like in a military regiment you endeavoured never to let your *house* down – *esprit de corps*.

We had four main *all-school* parties, namely, Christmas, St Valentine's, Midsummer, and Hallowe'en. It would be a fair bet to say that apart from Christmas most of us had never ever celebrated the other three.

It was quite a responsibility: your *spare time* (from the little you could scrape together) hovered around plotting and planning, in great secrecy. The main object was to give everybody a huge pleasant surprise! Nobody, but nobody, was permitted to have a whiff of what arrangements *your party plans* entailed, not even if there was friendly judicious (metaphorically speaking) arm-twisting. Surprisingly, one learnt to fob people off so well that rumours abounded which bore no relation to the planned festivities. Rumour begat rumour until the whole school was abuzz!

The American Air Force were our guests of honour one Christmas. The house giving the party worked like the blazes, planning their menus and cooking cakes.

The lighting, seating, decorations and entertainment – the whole caboodle – was undertaken by the house delegated for the Christmas party. In between schoolwork, compulsory games and evening prep we worked and played hard at school!

Word flew round on wings that the Americans were coming from Greenham Common Airbase – the base used for their aeroplanes and men in the Second World War just a few years or more earlier! The female of the species mistakenly thought we were going to be *like film stars*! They were Americans bringing presents! Wow and double wow!

Compulsory Saturday outdoor games (that day) had a lot of female *lingerers*: girls who had their hair in curlers underneath scarves hung back determined not to venture into inclement weather without their curlers and scarves. Somehow – nobody knows *how* it just conveniently *happened*! – the games teacher for lacrosse accompanied some of our *unscarved* girls out of the covered way, talking animatedly to them about nothing in particular. It had been a ruse on our part to get her on the games field before she saw the *scarved* girls! It worked! They had been hidden in the downstairs lavatories; now they followed everybody else on to the field, and by that time it was too late to send *the scarved* girls back to their dormitories to remove their *offending* curlers and scarves! The murky damp English weather was typical that day – those who'd not had the *courage* to wear banned curlers and headscarves were to rue it! That was the only rebellion of such magnitude which I can remember. It was made doubly worse because the boys running out to the football pitch had to pass the *rebels* and made fun of their curlers and scarves! All good clean fun!

Oh, the fluttering of young susceptible innocent hearts at the mere thought of us girls hobnobbing with mortals from the land of Hollywood! The only men we normally hobnobbed with were our fellow pupils, the teachers and the outdoor staff. Our excitement and *hunger* for other members of the opposite sex played havoc with our arrangements for the party. Everybody wanted the showers with much happy jostling and silly female inconsequential chatter. It was glorious fun and we remembered it long after the happy event.

That Saturday morning we had lovingly laid out our party gowns and underwear and myself my precious nylons (from my sister) on our beds. Our *own* shoes were well polished. There was such a rush to get to the bedrooms after compulsory games that we temporarily, good-naturedly, blocked the *fire-escape* staircase, which was the one in general use to reach our floors. The concrete steps had never had so many feet pound them unceasingly. Halfway up were the boys' doors, and they teasingly blocked us off from our next staircase knowing we were in a hurry to get titivated for the party. It was almost a case of lacrosse sticks and muddy football boots *at dawn* (duel).

My eldest sister, Emmie, had made my beautiful taffeta dress, posting it to me from America. She was a very talented seamstress. It was *brand new* and all mine in the *new* fabric, taffeta, *shot* with a watermark in the material. I gazed ecstatically at it hanging on a hanger from the door of the wardrobe. My beating heart almost burst with pride, rapture and delight at having a *brand-new* party dress, not a second-hand or hand-me-down one! I stood there and lovingly stroked its full skirt and touched the red satin piping on the sleeves, collar and waist. Then, like my bedroom mates, I slapped on a cheap face pack from a powdery mixture which had been mixed with water. Then we lay on our beds for twenty minutes, as the packet instructed, not daring to smile and almost afraid to breathe! It would have been calamitous had the *mask* cracked before it had turned us from ugly ducklings into swans, *hopeful* of a Hollywood film contract!

The smell was obnoxious, and we looked like we had slapped on thick brown mud, but the salesgirl in Woolworth's had assured us they were the best *cheap* face packs going! She should have known, shouldn't she? And we were none the wiser: we never had a vast selection of women's magazines at boarding school. We learnt as best we could, which isn't saying much for our *sophistication*!

Never could there have been a more innocent bevy of females than us Mary Hare girls (young ladies).

The bedroom resembled a snowstorm with the scent of all kinds of talcum powder sloshed liberally over young nubile bodies: damask rose, sweet violets, honeysuckle, lily of the valley . . . Our room stunk like a *tart's boudoir*. If you had said that to us we would not have known what you meant, we were *that innocent*! Faces were *pansticked*, lips reddened or pinked, perfume dabbed discreetly on wrists and throats and a little bit on a piece of cotton wool tucked into our bras! We did not wear our cumbersome hearing aids – it would have *ruined the effect* of our extensive toilette!

Roll-ons were struggled into or lightweight corsets or garter belts according to how slim one was. As a ten-and-a-half-stone plump damsel I groaningly hooked myself from waist to thigh, attaching thick pinkish suspenders to my precious pair of nylons. With my dress, my dear sister Emmie had included a brand-new brooch – my heart almost burst with happiness. One bedroom mate had loaned me a pair of red high-heeled shoes matching the piping of my dress.

This was an extra-special occasion, so we had express permission to use the main staircase of carved and panelled wood. Looking like the young ladies we actually were, but inside us we were still very young children trying to appear soignée, we trailed slowly and gracefully down the posh staircase, hearts aflutter, one hand on the balustrade, or bannisters, hoping to convey the possibility of our being *suitable for films*!

Giggling, laughing, we made it to the hall at the bottom of the staircase, lining up with the other students to *meet the Americans*. They, poor fellows, had to shake hands with each of us. My lot from my bedroom vowed we would never wash *that* hand again!

There was a small select number of tall men in their smart American uniforms, including their padre. We shook hands with the padre and officers who had accompanied him in the Jeeps. Receiving our share of goodies, including home-made American ice cream, had our faces wreathed in smiles – especially the boys'. Ice cream was a luxury in postwar Britain. This was one of our best Christmas parties. Hollywood would have been hard to beat us for *looks* that day! There were some awfully pretty girls at the school in my time. After the party, which went on *later than usual*, ecstatic starry-eyed *girls* tumbled into bed. We knew we had to rise for compulsory church service in the morning! The boys had to feed the pigs. The Rabbit Club members had to feed the rabbits and muck out their cages.

That night I was glad not to be a member of either!

When it was the turn of yellow house, St John of Beverley (my house) decided to have a competition for the best face mask at our Valentine party. I painted a beautiful poster and offered *all manner of bribes* for a good turnout of entries. I tied with Eleanor – she drew and painted a fantastic artistic creation. Eleanor was gifted with a pencil and paper besides her undeniable talent in Scottish dancing.

My mask was made with material and beads – my capability with a sewing needle stood me in good stead.

Whenever I see Scottish dancing I always think *visually* of Eleanor and Graham performing the Scottish sword dance. Neither could hear. They counted all their steps to keep the rhythm.

Sports days were important days at school, with rivalry between the houses to gain the Victor or Victrix Ludorum Cup. The whole day was akin a P. G. Wodehouse novel scenario – a similar ambience prevailed over our extensive fields and the old mellow building of Arlington Manor, with the letter *J* for Lady Jeune visible on the stone urns by the steps of the lily-covered fish pond, the bowling lawn mowed to *velvet* standard, plus the huge sports field. Tranquillity! An old-fashioned pleasant English day, for ever to remain in fond memories in our twilight years to come. How fortunate we were to be educated in such splendid surroundings. It was a joy to be alive and the weather couldn't have been more perfect.

From the main stone summerhouse with its *memories* of other generations long gone from the world we served little fancy cakes, made in cookery classes, a plethora of sandwiches and tea from the huge urn. I liked to imagine ladies and gentlemen of past eras smiling down on us as we were running, sprinting, throwing the javelin, putting the shot, and taking part in other athletic pursuits dear to our hearts in this beautiful land of ours amongst the green fields of all our yesterdays.

The girls were in their dark-green divided short skirts called *shorts* and white Aertex blouses. The boys were in white duck drill shorts and Aertex shirts, white socks and white plimsolls. What a magnificent sight we made marching round the fields in our groups of house colours, just like the Olympics! Many parents, visitors and special guests cheered, clapped and thought how well turned out we were – a credit to Miss Mary Hare's memory.

We had our coloured house sashes looped over one shoulder across our chests so nobody could mistake *which* house we represented.

I recall Ralph D., who was very good at sports and highly academic (one of our first two university students), won the Victor Ludorum Cup. Another year Alan won the senior boys Victor Ludorum Cup; the junior winner was David C. The senior victrix was Dorothy and the junior victrix was Diane.

I would have to write a hefty tome if I was to write *everything* about my schooldays at the Manor House.

I used to go to the South East Berkshire School of Technology twice a week for extramural studies on my own. Having to catch a bus there and back was quite an adventure in my hitherto sheltered life. Failing to be there on time meant a very long wait for another bus – our school was actually out in the countryside.

I learnt how to make pattern blocks and had to make a blouse with hand-stitched pintucking in a pale-lilac-coloured material as part of my City and Guilds Examination in Dressmaking, which I managed to pass quite well. With other (non-MHGS) people and the course teacher from the South East Berkshire School of Technology I went to London, where our work was on show at an exhibition of sewing and needlework.

I left school in 1953 and the Civic Centre at Dagenham, Essex, sent me a letter, which I still have. It says:

12th October 1953

Dear Miss Humphreys,
    The Committee have watched with great interest your school career and were delighted when you obtained a place at the Mary Hare Grammar School.
    Your recent success in the General Certificate of Education was reported to them last Friday and I was instructed to write to you and express their appreciation of the way in which you have made the best of your opportunities and to convey their congratulations on a good examination result.
    Yours sincerely,

I now come to the end of my school saga and the first volume of my autobiography. If I have inadvertently said anything upsetting to anybody please accept my abject apologies. Over the mists of time some memories change. I have done the best I could recall.

I am sure Miss Mary Hare would have approved of our happy schooldays.

With love and happy memories this book of mine is written. Our yesteryears, full of nostalgic *happenings*, *stories* and *incidents* of a long-gone age, are still relevant to us individually and collectively, recalling splendid teachers, fellow pupils, friends and relatives, all of whom I was fortunate to meet along the *highways and byways* of life in this wonderful country of ours.

Yes! There have been tears. Life is for living. God helps those who help themselves.

In the words of our old school hymn:

> *'They reap not where they laboured;*
> *We reap what they have sown.*
> *Our harvest may be garnered*
> *By ages yet unknown.'*

It has been a long journey, very eventful. I am glad I made that journey. Miss Mary Hare and our deceased tutors must be looking down on us with pride. We did not fail – their faith is in us. We are all well-educated deaf people, well-rounded individuals, an unseen umbilical cord binding us together – witness the well-attended reunions since 1946! I wonder if that can be said of many hearing schools and hearing students?

It has been proved without a doubt that deaf children are educable to higher standards than was dreamed of by Miss Hare and her colleagues, or by those who followed those pioneering tutors. The present generation of MHGS pupils obtain each year even greater academic achievements. The standards of present and past university-educated Old Hares is mind-boggling!

Within living memory it was the considered opinion of the great and the good that deaf people should be institutionalised and *taken care of*. How wrong they have been proved! Within living memory it was assumed deaf people should not marry and have children because deaf parents were not deemed capable of caring for children. To add insult to injury, it was said their offspring would be *deaf and dumb* (nasty words!) or of low intelligence! This was the icing on the cake in the minds of those *self-styled experts of the great and the good*.

Here's a thought for doubting Thomases and their ilk. How many times have you read in tabloids or broadsheets or seen on television news of a *deaf mother* abandoning or abusing a child? I am in my eighties and I have no recollection of such a harsh scenario!

You will find, if you did a survey in Great Britain, that most deaf people have/had hearing parents!

Yes, there are exceptions in some families.

Our offspring have normal hearing children of their own – generally speaking. Our offspring have done well in their careers; in turn our grandchildren follow academic and managerial paths. They are professionals in their chosen walks of life. Ditto the grandchildren, many of whom are professionals too in their chosen careers, ad infinitum. Some ignorant (and there still are some!) persons moan about deaf people having deaf children; I tell them of Graham in Scotland and his wife, who have three university-educated sons. Two are medical doctors (GPs)!

The embarrassment on the face of the ignorant person (or persons) is a joy to behold! They hum and they hah and they haw, "Er, um, er, um, I mean real deaf people's children!"

I reply, "Well, you can't get more real than that."

Wouldn't it be wonderful if someone did a survey of the offspring and grandchildren of Old Hares just to happily prove my points!

ADDENDUM – 2018

In my generation there were no interpreters, no note-takers, no helpers and no modern gadgets and media to aid any of us after we left higher education and entered the world at large.

We sank or swam under our own steam and Herculean efforts to enter professions and lines of work which hitherto had not been available to the deaf, and that included universities and colleges.

Sir Fred Clarke said in a speech given on an MHGS speech day, "We are trying to liberate the innate intelligence which lies within so many deaf children. With this liberation we hope for increased opportunities for the individuals. And, also, that our old pupils may go forth and be like unto the leaven which a woman hid in three measures of meal: until the whole was leavened."

Mary Hare, the founder of our school, proved by her pioneering work that the deaf were and are educable.

To this laudable truth I would like to add here some of the achievements of several people of my generation at the Mary Hare Grammar School, as it was then, after they left school and stood on their own two feet – in no particular order and in their own words with permission to use their full names.

To this I would wish to add that it is terribly hard nowadays for the deaf in general, especially those who have not had the fortune to be highly educated. Many find the search for employment deeply frustrating; many, but not all, end up living on benefits.

The core jobs of remunerative and beneficial work have gone overseas; trades have disappeared into thin air. Many school-leavers are without a command of English and maths. It is the bitter truth in this day and age.

A SMALL SAMPLE OF SOME ACHIEVEMENTS OF FORMER MARY HARE GRAMMAR SCHOOL PUPILS OF THE 1946–1950s GENERATION, BEFORE COUNSELLING OR MODERN MEDIA

(Per oculos non aures)

TONY BOYCE
- Fellow of the Gemmological Association (FGA), 1972, Berkshire.
- BSC degree in maths and physics, 1961.
- Chess champion, 1961.
- Qualified teacher of the deaf, 1967.

Tony graduated a long time ago, but had no tutorial help or interpreters or Internet or even any support at all!

BRYAN DISS
'I had an enjoyable job, but lack of a degree held me back in later life. Mary Hare did not help me with career guidance and I had no help at all after leaving, but I had moderate financial success and with my wife raised a lovely family.'

Bryan became deaf at age seven.

DAVID HIRSHMAN
With VSO he went to Namibia to work in a school for the deaf for three years. There he tried to involve deaf sign language in the national curriculum.

IAN STEWART
- Qualified quantity surveyor.
- Associate Member of the Royal Institute of Chartered Surveyors (ARICS).
- Qualified teacher for Teaching Deaf Adults in Further and Adult Education (ESOL).
- Lecturer in Deaf Sign Theatre for the Theatre of Arts Education and Deaf Studies (Hons) Course at Reading University.

Ian has written two books: *Mary S. Corbishley, MBE, 1905–1995: The founder of Mill Hall School for the Deaf in Cuckfield* and *My Years with the British Theatre of the Deaf, 1963–1977.*

ELAINE LAVERY

- The first female deaf lay reader in the Church of England.
- Auxiliary nurse on the children's wards at two large London hospitals for eleven years. 'I was told at first it would be impossible but thanks to two understanding matrons I was successful.'
Elaine became deaf at seventeen months (pre-lingually).

VICTOR MARKHAM

Victor left school in the fourth form because they did not think he would be successful at O levels. He sorted himself out at evening classes.

- Obtained an ONC in mechanical engineering after attending day-release classes. He had no help in the classroom and could not lip-read the tutors.
- Career in civil engineering design.
- Engineer in civil engineering products.
- Civil design engineer in electrical and mechanical engineering products.
- ONC and HNC.

COLIN ROBB

Deaf like his sister from a bomb in the Second World War, Colin was five years of age when he lost his hearing.

- Worked at British Aerospace as a metallurgist for forty years. He retired before the age of sixty.
- Name published in *Who's Who of British Engineers*, 1982. Colin's professional interests include fractography, standardisation and manufacturing processes development.
- AMCST.
- FIMM.C. ENGINEERING.
- Member of the Manufacturer's Institute.
- Freckleton (Lancashire) Parish Councillor, 2003–16.
- He wrote a *Metals Data Book*, published in 1987 by the Institute of Metals (ISBN: 0 90 4357 694).
- He went part-time to UMST (University of Manchester of Science and Technology) whilst employed at British Aerospace. LIM. AIM. MIM.

VIOLET FOOT

- First jobs: the Reader's Digest Association, 7–10 Old Bailey; Works Catalogues Library, Plessey's Engineering (temp); Spratt's of Bow Road (clerical); various factories (temp) as a flat machinest on shirts, blouses, ladies' clothes, men's overalls, etc.
- Started family – outdoor machinist, blouses.
- The number 1 RNID Certificate teaching lip-reading to adults.
- Member of the National Association of Teachers in Further and Higher Education (NATFHE), Newham College.
- LHRAC for technological education part-time teachers in adult education.
- Associated Examining Board GCE in British and social economic history (1968).
- East Ham (Newham) Libraries for fourteen years as a library assistant.
- First deaf Churchill Fellow, 1972.
- *Woman's Hour* interview on the radio.
- Harlech Television, Bristol.
- Thames Television to honour Winston Churchill's 100th anniversary.
- Successful author under the pen name Violet Frederick Foot (ISBN 0-7505-1952-5).

BARRY BLACKWELL

The Youth Employment found Barry a vacancy in the costs office of a small sheet-metal-pressing engineering firm. He worked his way up and became second in charge of the office in five years. He also did wages when others were off or on holidays. The director told him he was the best one in the office and suitable to be in charge, *but* could not promote him because of his deafness and inability to use a phone. He stayed at the firm for forty-eight years. It was a good firm to work for, but his deafness precluded him from higher promotion.

CHARLES BARKER

- C11 Eng. M. I. Mech. E.
- Registered with the Fédération Européenne des Associations Nationales d'Ingénieurs.
- Fully qualified design engineer and principal technologist for the Advanced Propulsion Department at Rolls-Royce, Derby.

JEANNE BROWN
- Member of the Society of Chiropodists.
- State Registered Chiropodist to the NHS – trained at the Birmingham School of Chiropody.
- Self-employed practitioner for twenty years before being employed by the NHS.

GRAHAM McLELLAN
Graham was a fully trained professional wood sculptor with a successful small private business creating commissioned wood-sculpture work, including a large wooden cross for a local church in Glasgow, in Scotland. He retired after forty years running his small private business, retiring a bit early.

GEORGE DREWRY
- Twenty-five years in the quantity-surveying profession.
- Changed career to become a qualified social worker with deaf and hearing-impaired people in Surrey for fourteen years.
- Ended up as a student adviser at the City Lit Institute Centre for Deaf Studies.

DONALD BROWN
- Scientist all his working life.